LUCY CALKINS, AMANDA HARTMAN, ZOË WHITE, AND THE UNITS OF STUDY CO-AUTHORS

The Conferring Handbook

DEDICATION

To Patsy Glazer, whose support and guidance has altered the landscape of literary education across New York City.

[v. 8]

FirstHand
An imprint of Heinemann
A division of Reed Elsevier Inc.
361 Hanover Street
Portsmouth, NH 03801-3912
www.heinemann.com

Offices and agents throughout the world

Copyright © 2003 by Lucy Calkins

All rights reserved. No part of this book may be reproduced in any form or by any electronic or mechanical means, including information storage and retrieval systems, without permission in writing from the publisher, except by a reviewer, who may quote brief passages in a review.

Photography: Peter Cunningham

Excerpt and cover from *Do Like Kyla* by Angela Johnson, illustrated by James Ransome. Published by Orchard Books, an imprint of Scholastic Inc. Text copyright © 1990 by Angela Johnson. Illustration copyright © 1990 by James Ransome. Reprinted by permission.

Library of Congress Cataloging-in-Publication Data

Calkins, Lucy McCormick.
    The conferring handbook / Lucy Calkins, Amanda Hartman, Zoe White, and the Units of Study coauthors.
    p. cm. — (Units of study for primary writing)
    ISBN 0-325-00612-1 (pbk. : alk. paper)
    1. English language-Composition and exercises-Study and teaching (Primary)—United States. 2. Creative writing (Primary education)—United States. 3. Curriculum planning-United States. I. Hartman, Amanda. II. White, Zoe. III. Title.
LB1529.U5C352 2003   2003019537
372.62'3--dc22

Printed in the United States of America on acid-free paper

07   06   05   ML   4   5

WITHDRAWN

TOURO COLLEGE LIBRARY
Kings Hwy

SERIES COMPONENTS

▶ **The Nuts and Bolts of Teaching Writing** provides a comprehensive overview of the processes and structures of the primary writing workshop.

▶ You'll use **The Conferring Handbook** as you work with individual students to identify and address specific writing issues.

▶ The seven **Units of Study**, each covering approximately four weeks of instruction, give you the strategies, lesson plans, and tools you'll need to teach writing to your students in powerful, lasting ways. Presented sequentially, the Units take your children from oral and pictorial story telling, through emergent and into fluent writing.

▶ To support your writing program, the **Resources for Primary Writers CD-ROM** provides video and print resources. You'll find clips of the authors teaching some of the lessons, booklists, supplementary material, **reproducibles** and **overheads**.

8/21/05

THE CONFERRING HANDBOOK

When I was a new teacher of writing, I studied with Donald Murray, a Pulitzer Prize-winning writer known as "the father of the writing process approach to teaching writing." Once a month, I would drive three and a half hours from my Connecticut school to the University of New Hampshire where I would confer with Don Murray for fifteen minutes about my writing, and then I would drive three and a half hours back to my Connecticut home. That year, I may have conferred with Don Murray ten times. I believe those ten conferences taught me to be a writer.

One-to-one conferences are at the heart of the process approach to teaching writing. When my colleagues and I work alongside teachers, coaching them to teach writing well, most of the time we are teaching these teachers wise ways of conferring with youngsters. Above all, we teach by demonstrating. This book and the larger book available separately, *Conferring with Primary Writers: Supporting a Month-by-Month Curriculum*, are our efforts to bring you in on those demonstrations. The units of study that accompany this book will refer to this book often, pointing you to various conferences that will be helpful to you at specific times in your teaching. Indeed, many teachers will want to read this book only as directed by the units of study books. Other teachers may find it helpful to quickly read through this entire book first to develop a sense of the entire year in conferring with primary writers.

The Big Picture

Whenever I am teaching a teacher to confer, I first try to help that teacher form a general impression of conferring. I often say, "Trail along with me for a moment as I confer with a child or two. Try to get the feel for how the child and I sit, for our tone and relationship, and for the rhythm of our interaction." I want teachers to see that conferring feels like an intimate (yet brief and productive) conversation among colleagues. I want teachers to notice that I sit alongside the child, with the child's work between us (but in the child's own hands). We are at eye level with each other. I ask the child to tell me about his or her writing, and then either the child reads me the piece, or I read it. Sometimes I struggle to read it and the child helps me, and sometimes I end up "reading" the picture only because the words aren't ones either of us can decipher. I respond to the content of the child's writing. I ask some questions that extend what the child has said. Soon I say, "Can I make one suggestion," and then I teach one point. I usually try to get the child started doing whatever I suggest he or she try. As the child works, I sneak a moment to write myself a note about the conference on a clipboard I carry. Then I move on to another child.

Sometimes I give teachers questions to keep in mind as they watch me. Does the child's energy for writing appear to go up, not down, as I confer with the child? Does it seem as if I am paying rapt attention to the child? Does the child talk as much as I do in the conference? There are other, more challenging questions than can be asked of a conference, but these are rudimentary, and the answer to each should, of course, be "yes."

The Architecture of Conferences

Although conferences are responsive, and each conference is unique, they nevertheless do have a predictable structure. It is not unlike the structure of a conversation between a doctor and a patient, a hairdresser and a client, a fashion designer and a customer: research, decide, teach, and link.

Research

Observe and interview to understand what the child is trying to do as a writer. Probe to glean more about the child's intentions.

The doctor approaches a patient and doesn't begin at once to search the patient's body, looking for ailments. Instead, the doctor inquires about how things have been for the patient. "How have you been feeling?" the doctor asks. Similarly, the first thing a good hairdresser says at the start of an appointment is, "So how have you been liking your hair lately? How has it been for you?" In the same fashion, a writing conference usually opens with the teacher asking, "How's writing been for you lately?" or "What have you been working on as a writer?"

Young children are not initially skilled at articulating what they are trying to do as writers, and so research often involves watching what the child has done and naming it. "Oh! I notice that you have sketched your story and now you are going back and adding labels," we might say. "I can see that you finished your story and now you are rereading it and adding more details into your drawing. You are revising your story by telling more," we could notice.

Usually we need to check what we see with the writer. "I can see you have written a whole lot of pages here. Are these all one story or are these different stories?" we might ask. "You say you are 'fixing up your ending.' Can you tell me more about that? Would you show me what you have done so far? What are you about to write next?"

Name what the child has already done as a writer and remind the child to do this in future writing.

When we study what a child has done, it is tempting to watch thinking, "What does the child need to learn next?" and "What can I teach this child?" This can lead us to take in what the child has done with a lens of looking for what the child has not yet done. Even if our goal is to move the child forward to brand new work, we will be most successful if we can train ourselves to take in what the child has done especially with an eye for the child's successes. It is helpful, therefore, to study what the child has already done and listen for what the child is trying to do with an eye towards being able to name something the child has done as a writer that we value and hope the child will remember to do always. If the child has added speech bubbles, I might say, "I love the way you have your characters—your people—talking and you include their exact words. That's just what writers do." If the child added color to her drawing, I might say, "You didn't just draw this any ol' way, you tried to make it special. Writers do that. They try to make their drawings and their words special." The challenge is to extrapolate from this one instance something the child should do again and again as a writer.

Decide

Weigh whether you want to accept or alter the child's current plans and processes. Decide what you will teach and how you will teach it.

The next section of a writing conference happens underground, as the teacher thinks, "Of all the many things that I could teach this child, what is the one thing that is apt to make the biggest difference? We are asking, "What will make the biggest difference not only on this day and in this piece, but for this writer and for all of his or her pieces from this day forward?" There is no one answer to this question. A teacher always has lots of options—the more skilled a teacher is, the more possible directions she can imagine for a conference. The decision is influenced by the child's intention. If the child was already trying to do something that we can help the child to do, then that is generally a wise way to proceed. The decision is also influenced by the curriculum—the unit of study. There are times in a unit of study (and early in the unit is usually one of those times) when we use conferences as opportunities to help children do what we want the whole class to be doing. The decision is also influenced by our goals for the unit and for the child and by our assessment of the child's progress as a writer. In the end, the decision about what to teach is also a haphazard one. There are lots of good options, and in the spur of the moment we choose one.

At this crucial juncture, we also think, "How will I teach this to the child?" and weigh whether we will teach by giving the child guided practice, by demonstration, by explaining and showing an example, or by inquiry. I discuss each of those methods later in this introduction. For now, it suffices to say that we decide on a method of teaching and usually, in primary writing conferences, the method of choice is guided practice.

Teach

Help the child get started doing what you hope he or she will do. Intervene to lift the level of what the child is doing.

We actually begin the teaching component of most conferences by telling the child, "I have been watching you write and I have one thing to teach you." Then we name exactly what we hope to teach the child. From this point on, a conference is not unlike a minilesson, and this serves as the connection phase of a minilesson.

We don't always use those exact words. Sometimes we say, "I have one suggestion to make." Sometimes we say, "Can I show you one thing that writers do?" Either way, we don't want the child to be left in the dark over the fact that this is the moment in a conference when, based on all we have learned about the child and the child's writing, we are hoping to explicitly teach the child something that we hope he will use often.

If I want to teach a young child to write, the best way to do this is usually not going to be for me to lecture. Instead, we often teach writing like we teach swimming. If I want to teach a child to breathe bubbles out into the water and then to rotate her head and breathe air in, I am apt to get into the pool beside the child and to physically help her to get started doing this action. As she does it, I offer some coaching tips. "That's it. Keep your ear in the water," I'll say. "Now blow bubbles, that's it."

When teaching writing we often get the child doing what we hope he will do and then coach into his actions in ways that lift the level of what he's doing or that lead him along to the next step. For example, if I want to show a child that writers reread their writing and think, "Does that make sense?" I might say, "Let me show you how writers reread their work. Let's reread this together," and then I back down and let him reread a bit of his text. Soon I intervene. "Now I think, 'Does that make sense?'" I say. "Does it?" I ask.

Link

Name what the child has done as a writer and remind the child to do this often in the future.

Of course, the goal is for the child to continue doing this work with less support from a teacher. Sometimes during the teaching section of a conference we encourage the child to keep going with less scaffolding from us. Always, at the end of a conference, we name what the child has done—repeating the teaching point, but this time, saying that this is what we have seen the child doing—and we encourage the child to continue doing this often, and in many pieces.

Kinds of Conferences

Most conferences have roughly the same architecture. It is helpful to realize, however, that there are a few main kinds of conferences. Early in the year, especially, teachers often hold ***content conferences***. In these conferences, the listener—and this may be a teacher or a peer—encourages the writer to talk in some detail about her subject. The listener listens raptly to the writer, interjecting in ways that nudge the writer to say more. "Wow! I had no idea!" the listener might say. "So then what did you do?" Sometimes the listener repeats what the writer has said. "So let me get this straight," the listener might say, and then retells the content in ways that spur the writer to add on. Soon the writer has said a lot, and now the teacher/listener encourages the writer to record what she has said. Often it is necessary to teach the writer a strategy for adding this content on—perhaps the writer needs to staple on a new sheet of paper, add a flap that can hold the new information, or start a new draft.

Early in the year, teachers also need to use conferences to bring children into the norms of a writing workshop. In ***expectation conferences***, the teacher may abbreviate the research phases of a conference. If a writer is leaning back precariously in his chair or writing on his arms rather than on the paper or hoarding magic markers and copying words from around the room rather than recording a message, the teacher need not spend much time researching. Instead, the teacher firmly and clearly lets the child know that his behavior doesn't match expectations for writing time and for writers. Then the teacher gets the child started on a more productive course. Often expectation conferences pave the way for a second kind of a conference.

At one time, we thought there were two other kinds of conferences: process conferences and goals conferences. But, in fact, almost always these conferences contain a mix of **process-and-goals**. That is, you might want to teach a child that writers often reread their leads, then get another sheet of paper and try to write an even better lead . . . but then you will probably want to give children a few hints about what makes a better lead. You may want to teach children that writers value details and add details into their drafts . . . but then you will probably want to teach children how writers go about adding those details into finished drafts.

Methods of Teaching

The fact that there are three different kinds of conferences—content conferences, expectation conferences, and process and goals conferences—is only modestly helpful because, at least when dealing with primary writing, the vast majority of conferences fall into the final category. Although it is interesting to know that you will teach both process and goals within a conference, this isn't enough to equip us to conduct an effective conference.

The vastly more helpful thing to realize is that in every conference and every minilesson, a teacher uses one of four teaching methods. Each of those teaching methods has it's own set of characteristics. In the conferences we describe, the teaching method is noted at the beginning and is cited at the point when that method is chosen. Once a teacher has chosen a method, the course that the conference will follow is set by that method.

For example, by far the most common method in primary writing conferences is **guided practice**. Once a teacher decides to teach using guided practice, the teacher knows the conference will proceed through some general steps. First, the teacher names what he will teach the

writer. Usually the teacher does this in a way that suggests this is a universally applicable lesson. For example, the teacher says, "After writers sketch our pictures, we label our pictures. We choose a word, then say it slowly. I will show you how." Then the teacher helps the writer get started doing what he hopes the writer will do. As the writer works, the teacher interjects lean prompts that either lift the level of what the writer is doing or scaffold the child's work in a step-by-step fashion. Then, once the writer has done the new work with scaffolding, the teacher lets the intervals between his prompts become longer as the child continues with less support. Finally, the teacher names what the writer has done and reminds her to do this often in future writing.

A second common method of teaching used in primary writing conferences is **demonstration**. The teacher again names what she will teach the writer, and she sets the writer up to watch her doing something. "Watch the way I study what this author has done in her lead and try to learn from it," I might say, and then I actually do the thing I am hoping the student will do. In a demonstration, the teacher doesn't talk about the activity or summarize the activity. Instead, we reenact the activity. We do it so the student can watch our step-by-step progression.

Once we have demonstrated for a bit, we pass the baton to the child. Sometimes the child can continue where we left off, sometimes we take the child back to the beginning and get the child started doing what we hope she will do (and now our teaching usually involves guided practice). In the end, we name what the child has just done (or started to do) and remind the child to do this often in the future.

A third common method is that we can **explicitly tell and show an example**. I think of this method as being a bit like giving a student a little speech about a subject. If we wanted to teach a child to focus his topic, for example, we could talk about how writers are like photographers and suggest that instead of taking a picture—or writing—about the whole meadow, a photographer is apt to focus on just three daisies, set against a stony boulder. Then we might give students examples of peers who started out writing about a broad topic—their cat—and ended up writing about a focused topic—when their cat got into a fight and came home with a bleeding eyelid.

There is a fourth method—***inquiry***—but we rely on this method very rarely with primary-aged writers. When using this method, we invite students to study something and to extrapolate the principles they need to learn.

Conferring is the heart of the writing workshop. Indeed, it is the very heart of teaching writing itself. Conferring is hard. When it is done well, it can change the course of a writing life forever. And the only way to become better at conferring is to begin; you can do that by working through the units of study and using them as guides in how to use this book, *The Conferring Handbook*.

PART ONE

LAUNCHING THE WRITING WORKSHOP

At the start of the year, you'll tell your children, "We're all going to be authors. Draw and write your story." Your children won't be entirely clear about the details, but they'll set to work, role-playing their way into being authors. Meanwhile, you may also feel as if you are role-playing your way into being a teacher of young authors! It's okay if you aren't entirely clear about the details of how one confers. When you work with your kids as writers, you'll tell them, "Do the best you can and keep going," and you'll need to follow your own advice.

Your first conferences will be content conferences. "What are you working on as a writer?" you'll ask. "Would you read it to me?" Then you'll pause to admire something the child has done—she added a detail, she wrote letters. Tell her, "I love the way you. . ." and name what she did that you hope she does often when she writes. Act interested in her content; repeat it in a way that elicits more. If you are responsive, "Wow! You brushed your sister's hair!" The child will usually say more. Tell her to add that— through drawing or through words—and help her start. Watch—and stay out of the way; let her do it as independently as possible.

You'll also teach children the norms of a writing workshop, communicating your expectations warmly and firmly through expectation conferences. Remember you are teaching each child to be a writer. "Writers don't draw on their arms," you can say. "Do you think Bernard Weber writes on his arm?!"

As this unit unfurls, you'll more consciously use conferences as a time to teach specifics of the writing process. "What I notice you doing as a writer that is so, so smart is . . ." you'll say. Then you'll switch, "One new thing I want to teach you is. . . ." Now you'll probably demonstrate what it is you want your youngsters to do and you'll help them get started.

As you confer, then, you'll hold content conferences, in which you listen responsively, elicit more, and help the child add the new content; expectation conferences, in which you induct youngsters into the norms of a writing workshop; and process conferences, in which you teach children the strategies writers use.

"What's the Story in This Picture?"

CONTENT CONFERENCE
METHOD: Guided Practice

Teach a child to draw representationally and to compose oral stories that accompany her drawings.

Research

Observe and interview to understand what the child is trying to do as a writer. In this case, the child is coloring in her picture.

After watching Bryanna busily coloring in the petals of a flower that looked as if it had grown to dwarf the apartment building that stood next to it on her paper, Zoë knelt down. "So Bryanna, how's it going? What are you working on as a writer right now?"

Looking at Zoë as if she should know, Bryanna pointed to her healthy flower and said, "Coloring!"

"Oh, yes, I see that you are adding color to your drawing. Can you tell me a bit more about your story? What's happening in your picture?"

"Oh, I was going into my house with my mom after school yesterday," Bryanna replied, continuing to color the flower.

Name what the child has done as a writer, and remind her to do this often in future writing.

"Wow, Bryanna! That is so smart of you to be telling a story from your own life, right there on this paper. Writers do that, you know."

Probe to glean more about the child's intentions.

"So, what's your plan for the rest of writing workshop, Bryanna? What else will you add to your story?"

"I am just coloring it," the girl looked at Zoë through the fringe of her bangs.

Zoë rephrases Bryanna's response in writerly terms— Bryanna is not simply "coloring," she is doing what writers do as she makes her story more colorful. Eventually, she'll add color to her words, not just to her pictures. Of course, Bryanna truly may be simply coloring, but Zoë wants Bryanna to see herself as an author, and so she describes Bryanna's actions in writerly ways. Zoë also asks Bryanna to "tell the story" that goes with her piece, even though it is likely that Bryanna has not yet thought of a detailed story to tell. Sometimes simply providing the opportunity to tell a story motivates the child to tell one.

Decide/Teach

Decide to elicit oral content. Do this by providing the child with guided practice in telling a sequential story. Be responsive by saying back what the child says and prompting her for more detail.

"Well Bryanna, you are so smart to be making a story here on the paper that is about something in your own life—but did you know that when writers make stories, they think about what is happening in the story? And then they show those things on their paper?"

Bryanna nodded, switching from red to orange. It was clear that she was focusing on her coloring project and not on what Zoë was telling her.

"Put the marker down for a second and look up at me, sweetie. I want to help you tell your story so you can put everything about it on the paper. That's what writers do!" As the child set her marker down, Zoë asked, "So you said you were going home after school yesterday—is that your building there?"

"Uh huh," said Bryanna.

Help the child get started doing what you hope she will do. In this case, help her tell the story of her text.

"So what happened first when you went home? Did you go up the steps there?" Zoë pointed to the zig-zag line that led up to the huge rectangular door.

"Yeah, and my doorman was outside because it was nice outside, and he waved to me and my mom."

Interject lean, efficient prompts to scaffold the child's work in a step-by-step fashion.

"Oh my goodness, Bryanna. Do you realize what a story you have here? At first, I just thought you went into your building and that was that. But there is so much more! First you walked up the steps, and then . . ."

"My doorman said 'hi' to me and my mom. Oh yeah!" she said, suddenly remembering, "He gave me a Tootsie-Roll pop. The red kind. I like orange better but it was ok . . ." she smiled rather wistfully at the memory.

Zoë has done enough research to see that Bryanna is not concerning herself much with communicating the important parts of her story on her paper. Zoë decides to focus on helping the child to first tell a more detailed story out loud, and then to record some of those details onto her paper.

When we teach the class, we often say, "Eyes on me, please." When the class has gathered and one child is speaking, we'll often say, "All eyes on [the child]." Young children are more apt to attend with their ears if they are also attending with their eyes. If a child in a conference isn't looking at us, pause and ask for the child's eyes.

When you hope a writer will say more, one of the wisest moves you can make is to give careful attention to what is on the page, including the drawing.

"So he gave you the Tootsie-Roll pop, and then . . ." Zoë prompted.

"Well, then we went inside the door."

Teach the child to record her additional content in a manner that seems appropriate. Take the child back to the beginning of what you elicited through guided practice, and help her get started putting this on the page.

"Wow, Bryanna. You have really got something there! Do you realize, when I first came over to have a conference with you, and I looked at your paper, I had no idea that all of that happened! You have got to put those things you just told me down, right here on the paper, right now! Writers do that, you know. We put all of the parts of our stories on the paper so that our readers can know even more about what happened. Let's go over your story again first—how did it start?"

"I went up the steps with my Mommy."

"And then?"

"And then the doorman said 'hi,' and he gave me the Tootsie-Roll pop."

Interject lean, efficient prompts to scaffold the child's work in a step-by-step fashion. In this case, help the child to record her story in the pictures she draws on her paper.

"So you said that you and your mom were going up the steps. Look at your picture. Does your picture show that?"

"No! Because I forgot to put me and my mom there!"

"You better do that, right now," Zoë said.

Zoë watched for a moment as Bryanna added her usual grinning stick figures, this time hovering slightly above the steps. Bryanna looked up at Zoë as if to ask, "Am I done now?"

"What else did you tell about, in your story? How about the doorman?"

"Oh yeah," she said, and added a third (slightly plumper) figure, complete with cap and buttons.

While Bryanna's story is simple, she has made great strides in telling it both sequentially and with more detail. Because Bryanna is not yet a writer who is ready to add print to her piece, Zoë decides to end the "eliciting content" phase of her conference with Bryanna and begin helping her record the details of this story on the page.

It is helpful to encourage the child to tell the story more than once to solidify the process that she has just gone through with your help and to encourage her to feel more comfortable doing this on her own in the future.

Often the difference between one person and another in a child's drawing will be features such as buttons and a top hat.

Link

Name what the child has done as a writer and remind her to do this often in future writing. Set her up to continue working.

"Bryanna, you have done such smart work today—when I first came over to you, I wasn't really sure about your story, because I couldn't see it on your page! But then, you told more about what happened when you went home from school, and now you are making sure to put all of those things on the page, so readers like me can know all about your story. That is what writers do. Now every time you do writing work, you can think, 'hmmm, does my picture show everything about what is happening in my story?' Great work, Bryanna. What will you add next?"

"My Tootsie-Roll pop!" Bryanna said, reaching for the red marker.

"You'll probably think of even more to add, knowing you!" Zoë said as she moved on to another child.

Notice that Zoë retells what Bryanna did today that is transferable to other pieces on other days. Instead of saying, "You added the doorman," she wisely said, "You told more about what happened, and then you added more to your paper."

Ideally a conference sets a child up to continue work for longer than the time it'll take to add a tootsie-roll pop, but this conference comes very early in the year.

"WHERE IS YOUR WRITING?"

Teach a child that during writing there's no option but to write; then help her listen to and record sounds in a word.

Research

Observe, interview, and recall your theory of the writer to understand what the child is trying to do. In this case, the child is devoting her attention to an imaginative game she's playing with her marker.

I watched Aja (a table monitor) efficiently do her job. She put the table's supply bin at the center of the table, found her own folder, and pulled a piece of writing from the top of the stack. Moving closer, I recognized the piece as one that Aja had begun the day before: the top half of three figures poked out of a thoroughly colored-in body of water. After rummaging around in the bin for a moment, Aja chose and uncapped a hot pink marker. "Hello, Pink," she said and then turned backwards in her chair and began hopping the marker up and down along the chair's backrest, with running commentary accompanying the marker's journey. I decided to approach.

"Aja! Let's talk about how your writing is going today," I said. "Aja, eyes on me, honey, I'm talking to you," I spoke firmly. Although Aja was obviously much more involved with the adventures of her pink marker than with my desire to talk writing, she did turn her head to look at me, eyes deep with make-believe. Her body still faced backwards, as if she was ready to continue her marker-play at any second.

"What is your writing work today, Aja?" I repeated.

"The Pink is in the mountains!" she smiled hugely. "He's going up into the mountains, bump, bump, bump!" She bounced the marker across the back of her chair again, for emphasis.

Often, our research begins with us watching from afar.

Earlier in the year, we need to socialize children into the mores of a writing conference. It's common for children to continue drawing while we talk at them. If you let this continue, your children grow up thinking that listening to you is optional and that they can tune you out if they want (just as they tune out the monologues of writers to their right and left). Don't let them grow up thinking that they can decide to ignore conferences with you.

Decide/Teach

Decide to redirect the child towards writing work. Explicitly tell the child what you expect her to do in writing workshop. In this case, help the child sit at the table like a writer and focus her attention on writing work.

"Oh," I said. "I see that you are playing a game with the marker right now. Aja, during writing time, writers work on their writing." I say this matter-of-factly. I speak firmly, but without scolding.

Help the child get started doing what you hope she will do.

"You have been doing such a great job as table monitor this week, and it really helps the other kids get ready to work because you are being so responsible about picking up the supplies. But you know, after you bring the supplies to the table, your writing work has just begun! Turn your body around and sit like a writer so we can keep talking about this."

Aja reluctantly turned her body around, still clutching the pink marker and eyeing it regretfully.

"I am happy to see that you have stories in your head, Aja. That means that you are ready to do your writing work. In fact, I see that you have a really interesting piece started, right here on your paper! So what will you do as a writer today with this piece?"

Sighing heavily, Aja looked at her picture.

Observe the writer: In this case, the child's attention has returned to her story.

* * *

Notice and Switch to a Process and Goals Conference

"Well, I was going to put labels on . . ." her sentence trailed off, and she looked with great focus at her marker.

It is quite possible that Aja is not in fact thoroughly aware of what her responsibilities are during writing time. It is also possible that she is aware that she should be doing writing work, but thinks she can fly beneath the radar for a while.

Notice that although I will tell Aja she hasn't been working enough during writing time, I also praise her industriousness as a table monitor.

Notice that twice already I've spoken to Aja about how to sit, where to look. It may seem like I'm obsessing about etiquette, but I don't think of it this way. I think we can't expect kids to intuit conventions we aren't willing to articulate. It isn't okay for me to confer to a child who has her back to me, and I need to say this clearly and early on so children grow up acting in ways that meet our expectations.

Sometimes our conferences contain two conferences, back-to-back. This is most apt to happen in an expectation conference. First, we stop whatever the child had been doing and get the child started, but then we often feel as if we need to give a brief conference to direct the writer well on the new work.

Research/Decide/Teach

Weigh whether you want to accept or alter the child's goal; in this case, decide to teach the child to write labels. You'll teach by giving the child guided practice.

Guessing that part of Aja's distraction with the marker might have been the result of frustration about adding words to her piece, I said, "What a great idea, Aja! I'll help you get started doing that, right this minute! I remember this piece from yesterday. What will you label first? The water? The people?"

"Well it was a *lake*, not water," Aja said.

"Well, then you definitely need to put that down in words."

I'm pleased Aja wants to write lake *because it won't be an especially difficult word.*

Help the child get started doing what you hope she will do; in this instance, remind the child to say each word slowly and to record the sounds she hears.

"When writers write words down, Aja, we first say the word really slowly, and then we write the sounds we hear. Let's do that now. Say the word, *lake*, slo-o-owly."

"*Lake*," said Aja. She had not taken my advice seriously about saying the word slowly.

Notice that I get Aja to say the word. I don't simply say it myself. It will help Aja to develop phonemic awareness if she stretches out words and isolates sounds she hears at their beginnings, middles, and ends.

Interject lean prompts to scaffold the child's work in a step-by-step fashion.

"You know how turtles move really slo-o-owly? Say it as slo-o-owly as a turrttlle moves," I said and joined her in saying, "*Llllaaak, Illlaaaak*."

"What is the first sound you hear?"

"Ummmm. Is it *l*?" she asked.

"Put down what you hear." She put down *l*—with the beloved hot pink marker.

"Now reread it. Does it say *lake*?"

Aja nodded, but without conviction.

Notice that I resist saying yes or no, signifying that the letter is or is not correct. I don't want to foster a dependency on me, and I don't want to get into a situation of correcting children's invented spellings while they are midway through a word. Another way in which I wiggle around the question of "Is that right?" is I sometimes say, "Can you read it?" and then follow up with, "So that works, doesn't it?"

"Actually, it says /llll/," I exaggerated the /l/ sound, thinking that a bit of silliness would make Aja more comfortable with my desire for her to hear and write more than one letter-sound.

I only tell Aja that she's written just /l/ because I believe she can hear and record more sounds in a word than simply the initial sound.

She giggled and said, "*LLLLaaaaaaaaaake,*" again.

"What else do you hear, Aja?" I asked.

"*K!*" she shouted and wrote a *k*.

Let the intervals between your prompts become longer as the child becomes accustomed to the process and is able to continue with less support.

"Reread it again, Aja. *Now* does it say *lake*?"

"Yep!" she decided. I decided not to push for the middle sound at this point, but instead to keep encouraging Aja's independence in the labeling process. I waited to see if she'd initiate another label. When she didn't, I said only, "What next?"

"*Sky,*" she said, and said the word slowly to herself, drawing out the /s/ for long enough to sound like she was impersonating a snake. She wrote an *s*.

She reread "/SSSSSS/," and smiled up at me. "Nope," she said, "it's /sssssss/!" She looked at the letters and began to darken the water.

"Is that *sky*? I asked quietly. "Say *sky* slowly like a turtle moves," I prompted.

"*Skkkyyy,*" Aja said and wrote an *i*. Then she began labeling the figure that represented herself.

Link

Name what the child has done, and remind her to do this often in the future. Set her up to continue working.

"Aja, would you remember that in writing time, we write. You are really good at checking your pieces and making sure you've added words, and you are good at saying the word slowly (like a turtle moves) and writing down the sounds you hear. Don't forget to reread, so you can make sure you put down *all* of the sounds you hear in the word, okay?"

"Okay," she agreed.

I could easily have said, "Now why don't you write sky," but I want to try to maintain a light presence and to do as little as necessary. This way, I can help children understand that my presence isn't any big deal and that they can carry on without me. It is crucial right now that I confer towards independence. Otherwise I will have a whole class full of children sitting around doing nothing while they wait for me to get to them.

It is important that we help children see themselves as the kind-of-people-who-do-school-well, and so I have been careful to support Aja's identity as a writer while firmly redirecting her activity.

"Let Me Show You How to Write More"

PROCESS AND GOALS/EXPECTATION/PROCESS AND GOALS
METHOD: **Guided Practice**

Teach the child to focus on his writing and to write sentences.

Research

Observe and interview to understand what the child is trying to do as a writer. In this case, the child is adding labels to his story.

Abie was working quietly, pausing every so often to check out his new lizard T-shirt. As I approached and noticed that he had added labels to the four figures he had drawn on his paper, he continued working.

Kneeling alongside his chair, I asked, "Abie, what are you working on as a writer today?"

Abie pointed to his work (a labeled drawing on a page with a still-empty line waiting for his sentence) and said, "This is when I went to the theater and in the play I saw a silver man and a gold man!"

"A silver man and a gold man? Wow! That sounds like an interesting play! Can you say more about what happens in your story?"

Abie said, "Sure. Well, the gold man and the silver man were walking around making jokes, and I was with my brother and dad. We were laughing!"

Name what the child has already done as a writer, and remind him to do this often in future writing.

I looked at his picture. "Yeah, I can see that you drew the three of you there in the audience. You are doing such smart work, putting those details into your picture. I hope you remember forever and ever that details matter! Is that your dad in the middle, the tall one?"

Abie grinned. "Yeah."

I open the conference by asking Abie what he was working on as a writer today. As children become more sophisticated, their answers to this question will change. Now Abie responds by telling me his subject. Within a few months, he will probably respond by telling me also his genre and, eventually, by naming what it is he is trying to do as a writer (for example, "I'm trying to show-not-tell"). One option I have now is to articulate for Abie what it is I hope he will eventually be able to say about his own writing. That is, I could say, "So, do I have this straight? You have just finished labeling your picture?" For now, I am content to leave well enough alone.

Pay close attention to their drawings. These are not superfluous. They are efforts to convey meaning—let them convey it to you.

Probe to glean more about the child's intentions.

"Abie," I said, "Can you tell me about the words you are adding to your picture?"

"Well," he said (looking at me like "I can't believe you don't know this yet"), "those are where I'm labeling."

"Can you read your words to me?"

Abie read, "*me* (ME), *silver man* (SV MN), *gold man* (GD MN), *dad* (DAD), and *brother* (BR)."

Decide/Teach

Weigh whether you want to accept or alter the child's intentions. In this case, decide to lift the level of the child's writing by helping him write more words. Teach by providing him with guided practice in writing not only labels, but sentences as well.

"Wow, Abie. Nice work with those labels. I want to talk to you now about something *else* that writers do when they're really good at labeling, like you are. Sometimes we decide we want to *say more* about our stories, so we write a sentence down here at the bottom of the page, on the line. That's what that line is for."

Help the writer get started doing what you hope he will do. In this case, help the child say a sentence out loud that goes with his story.

"Could you think of a way to tell readers that you went to the play? Could you say it in a sentence?"

Observe the writer. In this case, the child has eyes only for his new shirt.

Abie examined his lizard T-shirt, pulling it out away from his chest and tilting his head in an attempt to see it right-side up.

* * *

Notice and Switch to Expectation Conference

"Abie?" I repeated, this time getting his attention.

As if to explain the distraction around his shirt, Abie said, "After I went to the play I got this T-shirt, and my brother got the one with the snake!"

Very often the pattern in the research component of a conference is that the writer teaches the teacher what the writer is trying to do, the teacher finds some new work that deserves celebration, and then there is a second effort to research the writer. This second effort is focused on the aspect of writing the writer has spotlighted.

This portion of the conference corresponds to the "connection" phase of a minilesson. I want to clearly convey to Abie what it is that I plan to teach and how this lesson fits into the work he's been doing.

First I suggest that sometimes writers decide to write sentences. Next I plunge forward, assuming Abie will, of course, want to do this. Your assumptions matter. If I'd asked, "Would you like to do this or would you rather not?" the chance of bringing Abie along would be less likely.

"Ohh!" I said. "You got the shirt *after* the play? So it doesn't go with the picture and words you already have here?" He shook his head, indicating no.

Decide/Teach

Decide to redirect the writer. Clearly communicate what you expect him to do during a writing conference.

"Well, in a writing conference, we talk about your writing and about things that have to do with your writing. So we'll keep talking about your story, right?"

Help the child get started doing what you hope he will do. In this case, help the child turn his attention back to his story.

"What can you say, in a sentence, about going to the play with your dad and brother?"

"I saw a silver man and a gold man!"

Observe the writer: In this case, the child's attention has returned to his story.

* * *

Notice and Return to Process Conference

"Ohhhhh, great idea, Abie. You can say so much more about your story if you put it into a sentence."

Help the child get started doing what you hope he will do. In this case, help the child say each word, record the sounds he hears, and reread often.

"Now you can write that sentence down right here on the line. I'll help you. What will you say?"

"I saw a silver man and a gold man."

"So your first word is?"

"*I*," Abie said and wrote it down. He looked at me.

Interject lean, efficient prompts to scaffold the child's work in a step-by-step fashion. In this case, help the child to say a word, isolate the sound he hears, record that sound, reread, and continue with the next sound. When he has written the sounds he hears in one word, help him move on to the next.

I nodded. "Read that."

He read, "*I*."

I hope my message is that if the T-shirt story doesn't go with the story of the play that Abie needs to save it for another time!

It is important to be straightforward about what is expected in a writing conference. So it's perfectly reasonable to say, "For now, in a conference, we talk about your writing." There will be times when you say, "When I ask a question, my friend, your job is to answer me," or, "You know what, when we talk like this in a conference, I don't want you playing with your pencil sharpener. I want your attention."

I name what Abie has done in a way that is exportable to another day and another piece. I could have said, "Great job! You are right to say, 'I saw a silver and a gold man,'" but that wouldn't have influenced tomorrow's writing as much as this sort of a celebration does.

"Okay, what comes next? I . . ."

"I *saw, saw,* /sssssssssssssss/ . . . *s!*" he exclaimed.

"Write it down!"

He did and looked up again. I looked at his paper. He looked down at the paper as well and said, "*saw, saw.*" He retraced over the letters and was ready to move to the next word.

Interject lean prompts to lift the level of what the child is doing. In this case, help the child hear and record more sounds in a word.

Notice the lean, direct prompts. We try to avoid being too talky.

I intervened. "Abie, remember how we've been stretching our words on the paper?" He nodded. "Can you do that now? Look down at your paper. Put your finger under the part of saw that you've written. Read it. That's it."

Abie put his pointer finger under the *s* and said, "*sawwwww, sawwww,*" which, with his accent, sounds like *sawr.* "It's an *r!*" he shouted.

"Write that down, Abie!"

Let the intervals between your prompts become longer as the child becomes accustomed to the process and can continue with less support.

I could easily have stepped in and said "saaawwww" slowly in a way that set Abie up to hear more sounds, but I know Abie needs to learn to say words slowly and that I must always teach toward independence.

We continued this way for a couple of minutes, with me asking Abie to reread and to continue stretching words out on the paper. At one point, after he had written "I saw a silver man (I SR A SVR MN), " he jumped up out of his seat and yelled gleefully, "Hey, I'm spelling!"

"Yes you are, Abie!" I said. "Now keep writing, keep saying more and stretching it out on the paper just like you're doing. Just do the best you can."

The fact that there is no r in saw is irrelevant for this kindergarten child at this moment. Abie is saying words slowly, separating out sounds, matching sounds to letters, and the r derives from the fact that he pronounces saw as if it ends with an r. For now, let the error go and focus on all he has done right.

Link

Name what the child has done as a writer, and remind him to do this often in future writing. Set him up to continue working.

After pausing, I added, "From now on, when you do your writing work, after you label, you can say more in a sentence on the line at the bottom. After this, be sure when you choose paper, you use paper that has lines, okay? Like this," I showed him a piece. "I'll come check on you in a few minutes after I talk to Lily. Okay?" Abie nodded absently, busy writing.

Remember that most conferences end with you extrapolating the larger lesson that can guide a writer not just today with this piece but any day, with any piece.

PART TWO

SMALL MOMENTS: PERSONAL NARRATIVE WRITING

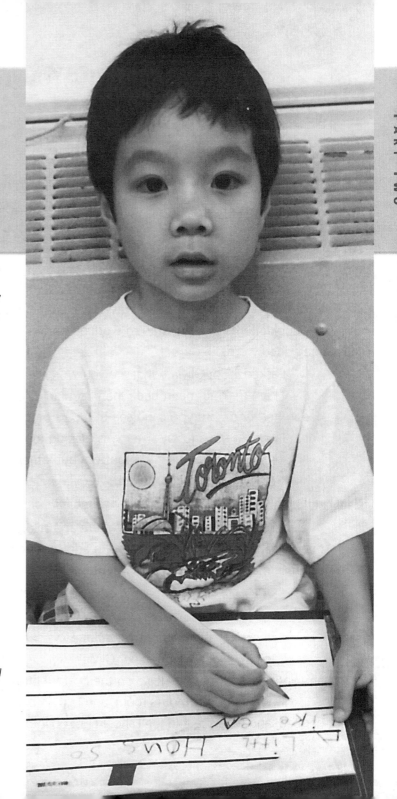

In this unit, there are a few jobs you need to accomplish in your conferences. First, you'll need to help a critical mass of children get the feel for writing small moment stories. Once half the class understands how to write focused, sequential narratives, those children can influence the others. Soon your teaching can shift to new areas. When you're supporting children in telling small moment stories, you'll be apt to ask:

- Can you think of one particular time?
- What's happening in your story? What happened first?
- So (retell what the child has said). Then what happened?
- Wow! So let me see if I have this straight. . . .
- Is this your story (retell it, touching each of the three blank pages)?
- So what will you draw here on page one?

Next, you'll want to help children who are not yet writing a lot decide which words to write and hear and record the sounds in those words. You'll provide a lot of support for this at first, gradually pulling back, making sure children can carry on without you. When you are supporting children in this work, you'll be apt to say:

- So you said this page is about (retell). What will you write here?
- So go ahead and write that right here (you point).
- What I do to write is that I say the word slowly and I listen for the first sound. Say it slowly. . . . What sound do you hear at the start? Write the letter that makes that sound.
- Reread it and keep going. That's it, put your finger under the word as you reread it
- What will you write next? Go ahead. . . .

In the conferences provided in this book, notice the rhythm. Generally, you'll ask, "What are you working on as a writer?" and take time to study what the author has done. You'll admire a particular writerly thing. Then you'll say, "Here's one thing writers do often," and you will teach, using one of several methods. Finally, you'll remind the writer that he or she can do this often in future writing.

PROCESS AND GOALS CONFERENCE
METHOD: Demonstration

Teach a child to plan, say, and sketch a story out across several pages.

Research

Observe and interview to understand what the child is trying to do as a writer of Small-Moment pieces. In this case, the child is completing a drawing on the first page of her booklet.

Olivia had sketched and was now coloring in a picture on the first page of her booklet. She had not started working on the second or third pages, nor had she added words.

I asked, "So, Olivia, what are you working on as a writer today?"

"I am making me in bed when I couldn't go to sleep. My mom is in her bed in her room, but you can't see that part on the picture. This is me in the top bunk. I was awake and my sister was making too much noise."

"Is that your sister on the bottom bunk there?" I asked.

"Yeah, she's kicking the bed!" Olivia exclaimed.

Name what the child has done as a writer, and remind her to do this often in future writing.

Laughing, I pointed to the picture and said, "I can see your eyes are wide open up there! Smart writing work to add so much detail!"

Probe to glean more about the child's intentions.

"So, Olivia, can you tell me why you have those other papers stapled onto your first page?"

"That's for what comes next in the story. But I don't know how it goes yet."

"So, what *does* come next, Olivia?" I asked, "You are in the top bunk, and your sister is making noise on the bottom bunk, and then what happens?"

"I went into my mom's room, and I got in bed with her. We were talking in her bed, and then she told me I should just go into my bed and look at a book, and

Notice that it is predictable that I start with this question. I know Olivia wouldn't yet be able to articulate her strategies, but I anticipate that as the year progresses she'll be more able to articulate her process and goals rather than simply telling me the content she plans to write.

When children are still at the stage when they convey a lot of their content through their pictures, it is especially important for us to respond to their pictures just as we do to their words.

When I retell what has happened thus far and ask, "Then what happens?" I am teaching as well as researching. I go back and summarize the story as she's told it in just the way that a more experienced writer might do for herself. She has

then I might fall asleep. So I went into my bed, and when I was looking at my book, I fell asleep! And then I woke up, and it was the morning, and I came to school."

shown that she can draw and then tell about her picture. But she may not realize yet that after drawing one page (one moment) the writer must ask herself, "What happened next?" and then continue on.

Decide/Teach

Weigh whether you want to accept or alter the child's current process. In this case, you decide to teach by demonstrating how she can rehearse for writing her story by touching each page and saying aloud what she'll write on that page. Set the child up to learn from your demonstration by naming what you aim to do.

"Wow," I said, "There is a lot more to your story than you have on your paper. So what I do, Olivia, when I'm not sure what to say on each page is I first try to go back to the start and touch page one and tell the story of page one, then I go to page two. I touch page two and tell the story of page two. Watch me as I do the first couple of pages, okay?"

Notice that I am using the teaching method of demonstration. In a minilesson, before we demonstrate, we tell students what we're going to, why we're doing it, and how we want them to watch. I'm doing the same thing here.

"Okay." Olivia had her eyes resting intently on me. She looked down at my hands as I gently took the booklet and looked at the page.

Touching page one, I said, "One night you lay on your top bunk a long time. You couldn't sleep because your sister was kicking the bed."

Help the writer get started doing what you have just demonstrated.

Turning the page and patting the blank paper, I continued, "And then, you went in your mom's room. . . ." I turned to page three and patted it, looking into Olivia's eyes. "Keep it going."

Now Olivia resumed the story, ". . . into my mom's room and crawled into bed with her. I went back to my room and looked at a book until I fell asleep." She added, "'cause, I was reading the book and I just fell asleep without knowing it!"

I help Olivia see that her experience is a story that has a beginning, a middle, and an end. I condense her long explanation of her picture into a tighter narrative line that is within her reach of being able to write. But I do this acting as if she's done all the work herself, and she willingly believes that all I've just done is to restate the story she invented. When we assist a writer, it is often helpful if the writer is fooled into thinking she's done the job herself! After all, this is the secret of training wheels.

Take the writer back to the beginning of the process you have demonstrated and help her get started sketching what she has rehearsed on each page.

"So, Olivia, we just did a rehearsal for your story. A sketch will help you remember it. We make a quick sketch on each page, then later we go back and add words and more details to our sketches. You already did page one. What will you sketch on page two?"

Olivia seems to have no trouble generating the content that will fill her remaining pages. I decide to make a second point, teaching her about sketch as a way to put her story onto the page.

"That's when I go into my mom's bed."

Link

Name what the child has done as a writer, and remind her to do this often in future writing. Set her up to continue working.

I said, "That sounds like a great plan! Start sketching what happened!"

Olivia looked concerned, "But what if I don't get done today? There's so many pages!"

"You probably won't get done today," I reassured Olivia, "But don't worry! Writers don't usually finish their pieces in one day."

"If you make your sketches today, and start writing your sentences, you'll remember the story you planned and you will add on to it. You can put it on the 'go' side of your folder." To double-check the "contract" we'd established, I said, "So what's your plan for the rest of writing workshop today?"

"I'm going to make a sketch of what comes first and then next," Olivia replied, "On this page is me in my mom's bed and on the last page, it's me back in my bed reading. Then I'll write it."

"What a great plan, Olivia! And every time you write, you can remember to touch your pages and say what you'll write, then to sketch it, then to write. I am so excited to read your story! I'll come check on how your plan is going later." [*Fig. 1*]

Notice that I don't elicit too detailed a story so that she doesn't lose her momentum in a swamp of detail. I would prefer it if Olivia dictated the exact words she planned to write (rather than talking about the content, as she does), but this conference contains plenty of teaching points already.

In fact, I often tell principals that when they are supervising teachers of writing, they should keep in mind that an indicator of a strong writing workshop is that children work on pieces over the course of several days. I want supervisors to expect to see kids "in the middle" of writing.

In the vast majority of conferences with upper elementary schoolchildren, we end the conference by asking the child to say what she will do next (and we record this in order to follow up on it). Asking children to articulate their plans is a less dominant structure in K–2 classrooms but still a wise option. I wish more of our conferences included this wise move.

I couldn't go to sleep.

I CONT GOTJLP

I went in my mom's bed.

I WT NMIMOMKBD

I read a book and slept.

IRDA BKNDCLD

Fig. 1 Olivia

"LET ME HELP YOU PUT SOME WORDS DOWN"

PROCESS AND GOALS CONFERENCE
METHOD: Guided Practice

Teach a child to listen for and record sounds in a word.

Research

Observe and interview to understand what the child is trying to do as a writer of Small Moment pieces. In this case, the child has finished sketching his narrative across three pages and appears to be at a standstill.

After sitting down beside Liam and glancing at his piece, it was clear to Abby that he was working on a true story. He had already sketched his story across the pages, but now he was fiddling with his pencil and looking around the room blankly.

Name what the child has done as a writer, and remind him to do this often in future writing.

"Looks like you have a great story sketched out there, Liam. What a good idea to sketch it first, so you have time for the words!"

Probe to glean more about the child's intentions.

Abby asked, "So, what are you doing now, Liam?"

"Well, I was writing about how I put the American Flag on my window and we couldn't get it to stay up so we had to go buy this special pole to put the flag on. . . ." There was a long pause, and then Liam continued quietly, "I can't write my words, though." He looked up at Abby.

When working with young children, our research relies on observation as well as on interviewing the writer.

Of course, it's not entirely clear that Liam was, in fact, worried about saving time for the words!

Decide/Teach

Weigh whether you want to accept or alter the child's intentions. In this case, decide to help the child label his picture. Teach by providing the child with guided practice in saying the word, writing the sounds he hears, and rereading often.

"You are smart to want to put words down, Liam. I'll help you." Abby continued, "Liam, you can write a word by saying the word slowly with your mouth and then writing down the sounds you hear."

"I want to write *pole*," and Liam pointed to the flag on his page.

Help the writer get started doing what you hope he will do.

Abby said, "So say *pole* slowly."

Liam said, "*Pole.*"

Interject lean, efficient prompts to scaffold the child's work in a step-by-step fashion.

"Liam, say it SLOWLY. *P-o-l-*," Abby said and swept her finger across the area where he would write it, making sure to sweep her finger slowly in the direction in which he would write.

Liam said, "*P-o-l-.*"

"Good. Say it again and think about what sound you hear at the beginning."

"*P-o-l*," Liam said, "*P-o-l. /P/ P!*"

"Good, write that." Liam wrote a *p*. Abby pointed to the *p*, "Okay let's read what you have written."

Liam asked, "*Pole?*"

Looking at and touching the letter, Abby said, "Actually, it says /p/. You want to write *pole*. Say the word again."

Abby is very wise to name the smart things Liam does (or almost does) so that they become part of his repertoire for another day.

Paper often acts as a graphic organizer. The three pages in a booklet help children tell the beginning, middle, and end of a story and the fact that Abby drags her finger across the page where the word will soon be written works in a similar fashion.

It is crucial to notice that Liam is doing the work. He is saying the word slowly, isolating the beginning sound. Abby isn't even doing it with him! For another child, she may need to join in doing this with the child, but she'll keep her voice quieter than the child and leave the child to do this sounding and stretching on his own as soon as possible. Abby avoids doing all the work for Liam.

Let the intervals between your prompts become longer as the child becomes accustomed to the process and can continue with less support.

Liam said, "*Pole /o/ /o/*" and said, "I heard an *o*." Although he said *o*, Liam wrote an *a* on his paper.

Then Liam again reread the word, "*P-ooo.*"

"Is that what you want to say? Po?"

Liam said, "No, no, no. I hear a /l/ at the end, but I don't know that letter."

Pointing to the *l* in Liam's name on the name chart, Abby said, "Is it like the /l/ in *Liam*?"

Liam nodded, added the letter, and reread the whole word proudly, "*Pole.*"

Link

Name what the child has done as a writer, and remind him to do this often in future writing. Set him up to continue working.

"You are definitely writing words, Liam. It's like you grew up and became an older writer! You don't just write pictures anymore, do you? Now you are the kind of writer who writes words."

"Remember, Liam, when your write words, say the word slowly, write the sounds you hear, then reread what you wrote. What will you write next?" To set him up for successful work, Abby added, "Will you write about the *sun*? Will you write *sun*?" She left after he began to work.

Abby knows this is an error, but she expects approximations and wants Liam doing the main thing with some independence. The goal for today isn't perfect spelling of one word. The goal is to help Liam see that he can, indeed, become one-who-writes, and that labeling parts of his picture can become part of his repertoire as a writer. Abby would defeat her purpose if she micromanaged to get everything right. Liam would learn to line up beside his teacher whenever he wanted a word written because that would be the only way to get it right.

Abby needs to decide whether to call Liam on the fact that just as he wrote an a for an o, he has also left off the silent e at the end of pole. She wisely remembers that her goal isn't perfect spelling. Her goal is to teach Liam a process he could use often to record more sounds in a word. She overlooks the missing silent e.

It's helpful to try to use compliments to help a writer create an image of himself or herself.

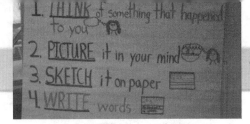

1. THINK of something that happened to you
2. PICTURE it in your mind
3. SKETCH it on paper
4. WRITE words

PROCESS AND GOALS CONFERENCE
METHOD: Guided Practice

Teach a child to revise by adding details to her words.

Research

Observe and interview to understand what the child is trying to do as a writer of Small Moment pieces. In this case, the child is adding color to a story that she sketched and wrote yesterday.

The class recently learned to "Sketch first, write, color last" to encourage them to spend more time on their words. Sophie was sprawled out, busily adding color to a piece she'd begun the day before.

"Hey, Sophie," I said, sprawling down next to her. "How is your writing work going today? What are you working on?"

"I'm adding color to my sketch from yesterday. Can you redo my pony?" she asked, holding out a handful of pink and purple barrettes and an electric blue hair-tie.

Name what the child has already done as a writer, and remind her to do this in future writing.

I gathered her tangled hair up into a ponytail, saying, "What a great idea to go back to a piece and see if there's more you could add. That's really smart."

Probe to glean more about the child's intentions.

"Will you read what you have so far?" I snapped pieces of hair that were too short for the ponytail with the five or six barrettes she'd handed me. She felt the sides of her head and began to read. [*Fig. 2*]

Most conferences in this unit begin with the child coloring. A few months from now, in the Authors as Mentors unit, not one conference begins this way. I considered revising these transcripts so they didn't all start so similarly, but realized this is probably a true reflection of what it is children tend to be doing when we initiate our conferences in October. Notice that we nevertheless begin by asking, "What's your writing work?" We don't say, "What are you drawing?"

It is yesterday when it was choice time. I was staring at them when they were making the flag.

Then I went over to them and watched. It looked so pretty.

It was clean up. It is all done.

Fig. 2 Sophie

"This is yesterday when it was choice time. I was staring at them when they were making the flag." She flipped the page and read, "Then I went over to them and watched. It looked so pretty." "Go on!" I said, as she looked up to make sure she had my undivided attention. She read from the last page, "It was cleanup. It is all done."

"Sophie!" I exclaimed. "I love that you wrote some words and that you've done such a great job adding detail into your pictures. What will you work on next?"

"Well," she said, pleased that I'd noticed the changes in her pictures. "I already drew in where our poetry books go and I gave Yvette some hair which I forgot to do yesterday."

"So what will you work on next?" Sophie shrugged.

Decide/Teach

Weigh whether you want to accept or alter the child's current process. In this case, decide that you want to encourage the child to add details through her words as well as through her pictures. Teach by providing her with guided practice in adding details to her piece.

"Sophie," I said, getting serious. "Did you know that when writers go back to a piece to see if they can add more details they add those details with words, as well as pictures? You can. . . ."

Sophie interrupted, "I *did* add words, see. I labeled the poetry books and I put in the whole alphabet chart, look!" Sophie indicated that she not only had a sentence-length caption on each page, but she also had some labels in the midst of her drawings.

Undivided, rapt attention is more important than any compliment could possibly be!

The drawings children make are often delightful and funny and incredibly interesting sources of information. It's easy for us to fixate so much on the words that we overlook the pictures, but it's wiser to attend to the pictures and to use the information we learn from them as we teach. In this instance, I need to notice her drawings. But meanwhile, she hasn't yet responded to my efforts to elicit her plans.

Help the writer get started doing what you hope she will do. In this case, help the child add her sentences on a new piece of paper.

"That is fabulous. It is always great to add more labels, but another thing writers do is we add *sentences*. As a reader, there are some things in your piece that are so exciting that I want to know even more about them. Like the friendship flag—that's what your whole piece is about, right?" Sophie nodded. "As a reader, I want to know *more* about it! You could write about that friendship flag."

"But I don't have any lines left on that page," Sophie said, warily.

Interject lean, efficient prompts that scaffold the child's work in a step-by-step fashion.

"Ah hah!" I said. "That's easy. Sometimes when writers want to say more about something in their piece, they can get a whole new piece of paper, write their words on it, and then put it in the place it should go in the story. Go right now and get a piece, quick, from the bin!"

Sophie hopped up onto her knees and "walked" on them over to the bin, a few feet away on the shelf. I chose to ignore, this time, the fact that she was traveling that way. She came back with a blank piece of paper (She knows from previous conferences that she is the kind of writer who will use three lines, and I wish she'd brought lined paper but I overlook this.). She attached the paper carefully to her clipboard and looked up.

"So, Sophie, what can you tell me about the flag so that your readers can get a picture of it in their minds?"

"Well, you were *there* when we made it," she grumbled. "You're even in the picture, see?"

I laughed. "Of course. *I* remember what the flag is like—it's even hanging right there above the green table. But," I said, solemnly, "how would I know anything about the flag if I *wasn't* there? How will readers picture it who don't know about this classroom and about how hard we worked on that flag?"

Children will resist our nudges, and it's important to persist a bit. Sometimes a teacher will say, "My children write in random letters" or "My children are just labeling." I respond, "Have you pushed to see what they can do with some support?" What children do automatically is not a great indicator of what children can do. Nudge, push, help—and only then can you learn what children can (and cannot yet) do!

I could have cut to the chase, by passing all the talk about what writers sometimes do, but I always try to extrapolate the transferable principles for the child. I'm trying to teach the writer, not just the writing.

As Sophie scampers off, I use the interlude to record some conference notes. If a young writer is going to need new paper, it's wise to gather the supplies during the conference. Although this can slow a conference down, the alternative is to end the conference with the child needing to get paper while still remembering our directions. Once the child secures the paper, the child then needs to reorient herself to the task at hand. Very often five- and six-year-olds get derailed along the way. Usually, therefore, it makes sense to get the paper in the midst of the conference and to end the conversation with the writer already starting on the recommended course.

Children take us so literally! Again, we need to not let a child's resistance totally sway us.

"Okaaaay," she said, chewing on her eraser and pondering for a minute. Then, looking brightly at me, she said, "I could tell about the things that we all drew that Yvette glued on!" She bent immediately and began writing, pausing only slightly between words, occasionally murmuring a word out loud several times. "It had police officers and firefighters," she wrote as I watched. [*Fig. 3*]

"That is *so* important. When you say more, your readers know more!"

Link

Name what the child has done as a writer, and remind her to do this often in future writing. Set her up to continue working.

"Today and every day after you write a piece, you can go back to your writing and add not only more colors and details in your pictures, but also add more words by adding sentences. You can add those sentences in where they go in the story. What is your plan for the rest of writing time, Sophie?"

"I'm going to write more about the flag, and then I'm going to tape it on here to the page by my flag picture."

"Great idea, Sophie. Keep going!"

When I went back to check on her later, Sophie had added, "And hearts and two suns. Now it is a friendship flag!" [*Fig. 3*]

This unit of study took place in October 2001, just after the destruction of the World Trade Center.

It is common for upper-grade teachers to end every conference by having the child articulate what she will do. This establishes a sort of contract. It's less predictable that K–2 conferences end this way, but still common.

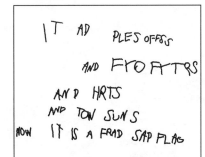

It had police officers
and firefighters
and hearts and
two suns.
Now it is a friendship flag!

Fig. 3   Sophie

PART THREE

WRITING FOR READERS: TEACHING SKILLS AND STRATEGIES

To prepare for your conferences during this unit of study, you need to remind yourself of the pathways along which writers develop en route to conventional writing (see The Nuts and Bolts of Teaching Writing*). You need to assess what a child can do, imagine the next step the child might be able to take, and scaffold that next step. Remember that you can't assess your writers' abilities to record words without nudging a bit. "Tell me about this page. What do you want to write here? Okay, write that right here." If the child needs more support, try saying, "What's the first word? Say that word. What sound do you hear first? Write that."*

Once you've pushed and seen what a child does in response, you'll have a good sense of what the child can do. In your conferences, you're simply going to help the child do work that represents the next step. If the child is writing with initial sounds, tell the child that writers listen for more than just the first sound, and help the child get started doing this. If the child is spelling every word by relying on sounds, tell the child that writers also think, "Do I know any words that are like this one?" and help the child get started doing this. You'll usually explain the new step and help the child do this new action. Halfway through your conferences you'll start the child doing whatever you decide to teach, then you'll interject prompts such as, "Reread it." "Point under the words." "What sound do you hear?" "Check it." And so on.

You must teach towards independence. In every way, get the child to do the work. If you say, "Reread it," let the child do it. If you say "Point under the words," let the child do it. If the child encounters difficulty, wait. Count to twenty silently. Give the child time to be active and to resolve his or her own difficulties. What you help the child do today, the child should be able to do tomorrow without your support. This will only happen if you expect and joyfully embrace effort, initiative, and approximation.

"Say and Record a Word, Then Reread"

PROCESS AND GOALS CONFERENCE
METHOD: Guided Practice

Teach a child whose writing looks like (but isn't) random strings of letters to reread and organize the letters into words.

Research

Observe to understand what the child is trying to do as a writer who aims to make her writing easier to read. In this case, the sentences the child has written to accompany her pictures don't have white space between the words, making them difficult to decipher.

Over the last few days, Juliser has asked Natalie many times, "Can you read this?" It has often turned out that Natalie cannot read these pieces, and Juliser can't read them either. When Juliser tells her stories to Natalie, they are filled with detail about the adventures she and her mother have together. But those stories can't easily be found in the print itself.

As Natalie watched, Juliser leaned low into her paper and began saying a string of sounds out loud, writing letter after letter in an unbroken line. It was as if her voice pushed letters out onto the page: "Itikwmimomeinrk."

Decide/Teach

Weigh whether you want to accept or alter the child's intentions. In this case, decide to teach the child to leave white space between the words in her sentence. Teach by providing the child with guided practice in rereading her words as she writes, making sure to leave white space between each word.

Natalie intervened. "Juliser, may I stop you?"

So often we see finished student work and can't make heads or tails out of it. The first recourse must be to watch that writer in the act of writing a sentence the child has just articulated out loud, and to look for what the child may be doing to translate spoken language into print. We need to notice both successful and unsuccessful strategies the child is using.

Natalie suspected that most of the letters were not random at all, but that in fact each represented a sound in the stream of speech Juliser produced as she wrote. However, Natalie also suspected that it could well be the case that one letter represented an initial sound in one word, and that the next letter represented a medial sound from a word much later in the sentence.

Notice that the research in this conference didn't involve interviewing the writer. When we know that we intend for our conferences to support the word work of writing, research usually involves watching a child write in our presence rather than interviewing the child. Young children can tell us they are adding on a new page or fixing their endings, but they are less able to tell us they are recording dominant sounds!

Waiting for Juliser's eyes, Natalie pressed on. "Juliser, I am going to ask you the question we have been asking each other a lot over the last few days. 'Can you read this?'"

Juliser began, "I took my mommy. . . ." Her voice trailed off. She looked to Natalie with the beginning swimmer look.

As soon as Juliser gave the beginning swimmer look, Natalie jumped right in with her. She said, "Juliser, what was this page supposed to say? When you said your story, what did it say?"

"It was about me and my mommy went bike riding in the park."

Natalie is keeping the words of the unit alive in the class and wanting Juliser to realize that the larger goal of what they'll do today is to write for readers.

If Juliser had not been able to recall what she wanted to write and could not find some hint of those words in the letters she actually did write, the first step would be for Juliser to tell Natalie about the picture. Talking about the picture can sometimes remind a writer of the message in the words. But in this instance, Juliser recalls her intended message, and the trouble comes only with the fact that she and Natalie could not match that content with the letters on the page. It makes sense to suggest writing the sentence again.

Help the writer get started doing what you hope she will do.

Repeating what Juliser said she wanted to write, Natalie said, "Okay, 'Me and my mommy went bike riding in the park.' Let's write it together. As we write, we'll go back often to the start of the sentence and read it again. Okay?" Juliser nodded.

Interject lean, efficient prompts to scaffold the child's work in a step-by-step fashion.

"So, say the sentence that you want to write. Say all the words," Natalie, said again giving a clear, brief prompt and then letting the child proceed independently. Natalie tries not to let her language overwhelm Juliser, and she tries not to do most of the work.

"Me and my mommy went bike riding in the park."

"Let's start with the first word. Say the first word."

"*Me*," Juliser said.

"Say that word again." Juliser said it again. "What is the first sound that you hear?"

"/Mmmm/."

"Good, write the letter that makes that sound." She did. "Read that." As Natalie spoke, she put Juliser's finger under the letter she had written.

"/Mm/."

It is comforting to Juliser when Natalie says "Let's write it together" and uses the pronoun we when she describes the work ahead. Do this if you feel it will help disarm an apprehensive child. Natalie has decided to teach Juliser that from now on when she writes, she needs to pause regularly to reread. When working with a child like this who needs lots of help, it is wise to choose one important and useful strategy to really learn rather than having the child learn a little about a lot.

"What else do you hear in that word?" Natalie asked, directing Juliser's finger so that it now pointed to the empty space beside her the letter she'd written.

"I hear /eeeee/."

"Good. Now write the letter that makes that sound." As Juliser finished recording the e, Natalie continued. "Read that." Natalie responded, "*Me.*" "Are those the only sounds you hear? Now we have come to the end of the word. Let's reread what we have written so far again. Remember we said we would reread often?"

Natalie took Juliser's finger and again put it under the first letter. Juliser read, "*Me.*"

Natalie said, "Let me see if *I* can reread it," and she put her finger under the word and voiced, "/mm/" and then proceeded to the e. "I can read it!" she said. "Yippee!"

Let the intervals between your prompts become longer as the child becomes accustomed to the process and can continue with less support.

"Let's keep going, okay?" Natalie continued, "We need to leave a blank space because we are at the end of a word. Now what word comes next?"

Juliser said "*And,*" and she and Natalie worked their way through to the last sound she heard in the word. Again Natalie reminded Juliser to leave a blank space and to reread all that they had written so far. Juliser did, and then they worked together on *mommy* and *went*, with Natalie offering less support. Again Juliser reread her message.

Link

Name what the child has done as a writer, and remind her to do this often in future writing. Set her up to continue working.

Natalie said, "Juliser, I know it feels like we are rereading a lot of times to get this page of the story written, but it is really important for you to keep rereading often as you write the rest of this page and the rest of your story. Remember that I will be sitting at home tonight trying to read your writing, but you won't be there to help me. You need to help me now by the way you do this writing, okay? What will your next word be?" Before Natalie moved on, Juliser said "*Bike,*" had written a *b*, and was rereading it.

Natalie isn't teaching Juliser a strategy that Juliser will be able to use on her own whenever she writes. Instead, Natalie is functioning like training wheels, allowing Juliser to keep going and to get a sense of what writing should feel like. When this level of support is needed it is especially important to work with the child every day. Because Natalie has so many children and almost all of them are struggling writers, she won't be able to get to Juliser every day during writing. Natalie makes an arrangement for Juliser to come to school early a few days a week and gives her extra time then. A few weeks of this intensive, continued instruction makes the world of difference for Juliser as both a reader and a writer.

Of course, it is a transitional step to ask Juliser to reread after she records each letter. In the end, skilled writers certainly don't do this. But we also don't read pointing under each word. Pointing under each word and rereading often as one proceeds through a sentence are similar in that both are temporary scaffolds that we may ask a child to do, knowing that we will soon tell that child that he or she doesn't need to do this any longer.

PROCESS AND GOALS CONFERENCE
METHOD: **Guided Practice**

Teach a child to reread, fixing places where a lack of white space makes the text difficult.

Research

Observe and interview to understand what the child is trying to do as a writer who aims to make his writing easier to read. In this case, the child has written some sentences and is now adding color to his Small-Moment piece.

After watching Fabio for a moment, I approached and asked what he was working on as a writer. He was filling every square inch of space on the paper with color.

"How's it going, Fabio? What is your writing work for today?"

"I don't know."

"Well, it looks like you are making a story about pumpkins. Is this a tiny-moment story about something you did with pumpkins?" Fabio nodded. We turned to the first page and admired together the three gigantic, red-lipped pumpkins he had drawn.

"Were you trying to reread the words that you wrote before, Fabio?" I asked, and he nodded. "Could you reread them now?"

We often begin a conference by asking a child to talk about the work he is doing as a writer. Some children, like Fabio, don't understand the question or have words to answer it. Some answer with their topic. ("I'm writing about pumpkins.") Some provide their topic and their genre. ("I'm writing a tiny moment story about when I got a pumpkin.") Our hope is that eventually a child will respond with topic, genre, and a description of what the writer is trying to do as a writer. ("I'm writing a tiny moment story about getting a pumpkin and I'm trying to add details that help you picture how big the pumpkin was!") When a child like Fabio doesn't have a response to the question at all, we use physical evidence of what he's been doing and try to articulate what we suspect he's working on.

He looked at the paper and read, "I went to the . . ." and then looked up at my face, repeating "I went to the . . ." two or three times more. His lower lip was beginning to poke out and his shoulders hunched—signs I recognized as sometimes preceding a brief but stormy cascade of tears.

Name what the child has already done as a writer, and remind him to do this often in the future.

"Fabio, it is so smart of you to try, try, try to reread your writing. Sometimes it is hard to reread our writing. I want to congratulate you on doing this hard-work-kind-of-reading. I saw you bring out your finger when you ran into trouble, and reread, and look at the picture to try to get help. It was really smart for you to work so hard at trying to reread your writing."

Decide/Teach

After observing the child rereading, decide to teach the child to leave white spaces between the words. Teach by providing him guided practice rereading, monitoring and repairing his white space.

"I think I can make rereading easier, Fabio," I said matter-of-factly. "I think you're getting mixed up here in your rereading because there's not a space between *the* and *farmers market.* Do you see? If you just erase *the* and scoot it over here, it will be easier to reread. Do that now, and then try rereading."

Help the child get started doing what you want him to do.

Lip still poked out, Fabio erased *the* and scooted it over, leaving a clear space between it and *farmers market.* "I went to the farmers market and I got my pumpkin," he read. After a moment, he looked me straight in the face again and said with wonder, "I forgot so much about my writing!"

Interject lean, efficient prompts to scaffold the child's work in a step-by-step fashion.

"It's good to put spaces between each of your words so it's easier to reread it and remember," I said. He nodded, lip back in its normal place, face calm.

"Let's look at the rest of your piece and see if there are any more places where your words are squished together," I said. "Because now you know how to fix that problem!"

Don't rush in to help every time a child is struggling to reread his words. The struggle is important. Also, don't be surprised if your children are sometimes on the brink of tears. Don't feel as if no other teacher could possibly have messed up as badly as you have, creating such discomfort. This has happened to us all.

Remember that whenever a child has done something that is partly "wrong," the child will also have done something partly "right." In this instance, Fabio doesn't succeed at rereading his writing, but he does succeed at trying hard and at using some strategies.

By looking for more places where Fabio can adjust his spacing, I give him more chances to practice what he has just learned.

Fabio read much of the next page with only one patch of trouble. After he deciphered, "That pumpkin was too heavy for me," he erased and moved *was* over so there was enough space between it and *pumpkin* so that "the kids can read it."

Link

Name what the child has done as a writer, and remind him to do this often in future writing. Set him up to continue working.

"Before you finish adding color, Fabio, check out the rest of your words to make sure there are spaces between each of them and to make sure that you can reread what you wrote. And when you start new pieces, remember, you can add spaces as you go, okay?"

"Okay," he said seriously, turning the page and beginning to reread out loud to himself, finger below the words.

PROCESS AND GOALS CONFERENCE
METHOD: Demonstration

Teach a child to punctuate.

Research

Observe and interview to understand what the child is trying to do as a writer who aims to make her writing easier to read. In this case, the child is writing a sentence or two on each page without using punctuation.

As Camilla worked, I watched her write a sentence or two at the bottom of each page, and I noticed her stamina as a writer. One page, two—she kept at it. Glancing at the text, I saw that she'd written about a pigeon with a broken wing, and that yes, indeed, I could read her writing. Noticing my presence, Camilla paused as if to say, "Do you want to talk?" but I motioned for her to continue.

Watching Camilla was helpful because it soon became clear that although she didn't use any punctuation at all, she did segment her writing into sentences, dictating what was clearly one sentence at a time to herself and taking a little rest from writing whenever a sentence was complete.

Name what the child has already done as a writer, and remind her to do this often in future writing.

"Camilla," I said, "Usually when I come up to you during writing, I ask 'What are you working on as a writer?' But today I came with one question in my mind. I bet you know what it was. I came asking, 'Can I read Camilla's writing?' Do you know what the answer is? It is yes. Let me show you," and I read a bit of it aloud. "I can read your writing, Camilla, because you know a lot of words like that," and I snapped my fingers. "That is a real talent! And if a word is tough for you, I can see that you use the words you know to help you with the words you don't know. Congratulations. Do that for the rest of your life."

I make a great point of not beginning a conversation right away because I want children to continue to work before my eyes. If I launch into a conference the moment I arrive at a child's side, then anytime a grownup pulls a chair close to a child, the child will automatically stop her work and turn to talk. How will we understand their strategies and habits if we can never watch children as they work?

I want children to become accustomed to the patterns in a writing workshop and therefore, when I break out from the norm, I point out that I have done this (just this one time). If a minilesson will go longer than usual, for example, I tell children that this will happen. Similarly, I point out to Camilla that this time, I didn't ask what she was working on or pay attention to the content of her story. This time, I came asking, "Can I read this?" and attending especially to her conventions.

Decide/Teach

Weigh whether you want to accept or alter the child's intentions. In this case, decide to teach by demonstrating to the child how writers use end punctuation to help people read their writing. Demonstrate by reading both a published book and her own writing with and without the help of punctuation. Set the child up to learn from your demonstration by naming what you aim to do.

"Camilla, there is one thing you could do to make your writing much easier for me to read," I said. "It is something that grownup, famous authors do." Then I opened a book she'd been reading and pointed to the punctuation. "I want to show you how, when I am reading, these periods help me know when to stop."

Demonstrate to show the writer what you hope she will soon do. In this case, show the child how end punctuation tells readers when to stop and take a breath.

Continuing, I told Camilla, "These periods are like red lights when I am driving. They say, 'Stop for a second, take a breath!' Let me show you." I began to read, placing my finger under each word and, in due course, under each period. I paused dramatically for each of the periods and took an exaggerated breath. Camilla giggled.

Help the writer get started doing what you have just demonstrated.

"You try it—let the periods make *you* stop," I said. Camilla then reread the same page, pausing just as dramatically for the periods.

Demonstrate to show the writer how it feels to read writing with no end punctuation.

"Now, watch what happens if we pretend that Bill Martin doesn't have periods in his writing," I said. "It would go like this." I reread the same text in a silly, words-falling-all-over-each-other fashion.

"What I noticed when I tried to read your writing (other than the great spelling) is that you forgot to put these periods in. When I first read this page, I read it like this," I said, and reenacted a silly, unpunctuated reading of her text.

Help the writer get started doing what you hope she will do. In this case, help the child read her writing, listening for where periods should go and adding them in.

"Will you read your writing the way it is *supposed* to go?" I asked. She did, pausing dramatically at the end of each sentence and smiling up at me mischievously.

In this instance, I notice that Camilla is writing easily. She has succeeded in writing a text I can decipher. The new direction I suggest in this conference is almost an arbitrary choice for me.

Notice first that I come right out and teach as directly as I can. I don't ask a million questions and try to elicit this knowledge from the child. I simply tell her what I know, drawing on whatever I can to make my point interesting and understandable. To highlight the one feature of punctuation, I discuss how the two texts under discussion would have gone had they not had the benefit of punctuation.

Take the writer back to the beginning of the process you have demonstrated, and help her get started putting punctuation into her sentences.

"So now, Camilla, you have been paying close attention to where you need to add periods to your own work, so it doesn't just keep going and going without giving the reader a place to stop and breathe! Now let's get started adding periods together."

We did a bit of this work together, and I asked, "So, can you keep doing this Camilla?" I recorded some conference notes while she continued rereading and adding punctuation. She added too many periods, sometimes using a period when in fact a comma would have been called for, but I let this go.

Link

Name what the child has done as a writer, and remind her to do this often in future writing. Set the child up to continue working.

I watched as Camilla continued work. When she added a period, I said, "That's it. You are doing it just like Bill Martin! You got it!" Then I added, "What you are doing is perfect. Keep doing this forever and forever."

Conferences such as this reinforce the connection's between reading and writing. Some students will be stronger in writing and learn concepts of print first through writing. Other kids pick up these concepts first through reading. Either way it is important to bring reading into the writing workshop.

I made a note to tackle Camilla's random mixture of uppercase and lowercase letters during a future conference. I imagine saying, "Last time we talked, we looked at this book and noticed the way Bill Martin used periods. You can learn a lot by looking at what other authors do. Would you look, for example, at the way Bill Martin has used uppercase and lowercase letters, and see if you can learn something without me even helping. See if you can learn from Bill Martin, because I bet you can."

PART FOUR

THE CRAFT OF REVISION

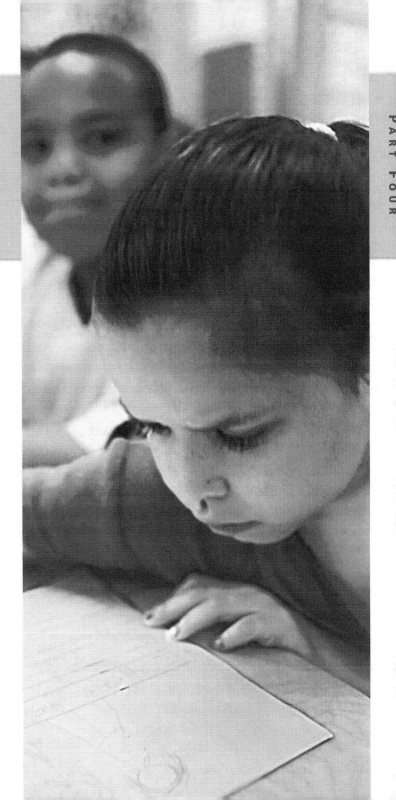

As children move from one unit of study to another, you hope that the instructions you've given in earlier conferences last and accumulate, giving your children an expanding repertoire of strategies to draw on. Similarly, each new unit should give you an ever-expanding repertoire of conferences to draw upon. By now, you should be able to conduct content conferences in which you lure children to say and then write more about their subjects. You should be able to conduct expectation conferences in which you clearly convey the norms of a writing workshop and get the child started living and working within those norms. You should be able to support children in writing focused, sequential, detailed narratives . . . and in writing in such a way that they and others can read their writing. You should be able to provide lean, efficient prompts that help a child write for readers.

In this new unit, your conferences will become dramatically more interesting. Because your children will always be revising finished work, they'll have much more to say when you ask, "What are you working on as a writer?" They'll always be doing something deliberate to improve a draft. As the unit unfurls, you can expect them to tell you what they are doing (adding on, altering a section, taking out) and why they are doing this (to add dialogue, to show not tell, to write a better ending).

You can teach processes or goals. Become accustomed to naming what the child has done that you hope will become part of the child's repertoire, and then to saying, "Can I teach you one thing?" Then try to teach in a way that will work not only for this piece, and this day, but also for another piece and another day. Be aware that you can teach by demonstrating a strategy you hope the child will try, or by providing guided practice in which you support the child as she tries the new work.

"THIS PART IS CONFUSING TO ME"

PROCESS AND GOALS CONFERENCE
METHOD: Proficient Partner

Teach a child to reread for sense and to revise to clarify the content.

Research

Observe and read the child's writing to understand what the child is trying to do as a writer and as a student of revision. In this case, the child has written a confusing story, but she acts as if her book is done.

From across the room, I watched Alexa carefully make the final page in her book. The centerpiece of the page was a design, and the rest of the page contained speech balloons full of good-byes. Then, as a final gesture of completion, Alexa closed the book and rubbed it down, back and forth, back and forth, as if she was pressing a shirt. By the time I'd reached her she was working hard to balance the completed book on her head.

Seeing me, Alexa didn't wait for me to ask the standard, "What are you working on as a writer?" but instead rested the book into position between us and began to read it, her finger moving along under the words. [*Fig. 4*]

I was eating my breakfast. My breakfast was bagel.

"See, I added a detail," she pointed out.

My plate flung up and my milk had a reaction to it.

"There," she said, and closed the book with firmness. "It was a real mess."

Name what the child has already done, and remind her to do this often in the future.

"Alexa, I'm glad to see you reread your writing when you finish writing it. Writers do that!"

I was eating my breakfast. My breakfast was bagel.

My plate flung up and my milk had a reaction to it

and my milk spilled and my Dad cleaned it up.

Fig. 4 Alexa

It's helpful to anticipate that your internalized conference structure will provide you with a space in which you are expected to name what the child has done that works well. Sometimes it's a stretch to figure out what you want to applaud. Push yourself!

Decide/Teach

Weigh whether you want to accept or alter the child's intentions. In this case, decide to teach her that writers need to notice and rectify any confusion their writing creates in their readers' minds. Teach by becoming a proficient (and confused) writing partner and by explicitly telling her that writers need to reread, monitoring for sense.

"Alexa, I'm not sure that I am understanding your story," I said, and I reread what she'd written, visibly trying to piece it together. I wanted Alexa to see I was struggling to understand her writing. "It is confusing to me. Let me try to get this straight," I said. Then, referring to page one, I paraphrased, "So you were eating your bagel. . . ." Then, turning to page two, I said, "And . . ." (my voice revealed my confusion) "and your plate flung up?"

Alexa nodded, "Yup, it really did!"

"You had a flying plate?" I responded, eyes big.

Help the writer get started doing what you hope she will do; in this case, you hope the child will clarify her story orally and in writing.

"Silly, silly, silly, no," Alexa said. "My arm touched the plate!"

"Oh! Now I get it! You've got to say that, Alexa, because I read this—'I was eating my bagel and my plate flung up,' and I thought your plate got wings and started zooming through the sky! That didn't make sense."

Instead of adding clarifying information onto page one as I expected, Alexa grabbed a new sheet and rewrote her first page entirely. Now instead of saying she was eating breakfast, her breakfast was a bagel, and her plate flung up, she wrote:

I was eating my breakfast. My arm touched the plate.

If the child's text confuses you, be sure to reveal your confusion to the writer.

There are so many moments like this one, when children enchant and entertain us and we find ourselves laughing aloud. But if we are also confused, it is important to trust that confusion and to call the child's attention to it.

We are giving children their first experiences of writing for a reader. We do no favors if we supply the missing explanations and fill in the missing pieces. Instead we need to reveal our experience of reading the text so that the writer can anticipate what will work for their readers.

Once the child has explained what she meant to say, remind her she needs to say this on the page.

When you nudge a child to revise, the child may simply start an entirely new draft. These are very young children and you will be glad for whatever they do, but bear in mind that if revision always consists of writing entirely new drafts, the child may not be revising at all. The new draft will often have a host of brand-new problems.

Explicitly tell the child what you hope she will do next (and often) when she revises. In this case, encourage the child to reread the next part and think about how to make her writing clearer by adding more details.

"Alexa, let me be your partner on the next page. Would you read it to me and I'll listen to see if it makes sense?"

Alexa read aloud, "My plate flew up and my milk had a reaction to it." Then she added, by way of an explanatory comment, "That means my milk got spilt."

"Oh!" I said, knocking my forehead in a well-blow-me-down fashion. "I had no idea what you meant by 'My milk had a reaction to it.' Now I understand!"

Alexa nodded, happy as a clam, while I waited to see if she would conclude that she needed to add that vitally necessary information onto her page. She showed no indication of doing so. I persevered. "Alexa, I am wondering if this conference is teaching you something that writers do a lot?"

"They gotta make sense."

"You are smart to realize that. And did you make your first page make sense? Read it over and think, 'Does this make sense?'" Alexa reread the first page—the one she'd rewritten—and nodded. "Keep going. Read your next page."

Alexa picked up her pencil and reread the page: "My plate flew up and my milk had a reaction to it." Now it was Alexa's turn to knock on her forehead in a well-blow-me-down fashion, and she began revising the page.

Link

Name what the child has done, and remind her to continue doing this for the next few minutes.

"Alexa," I said. "When I told you part of your story was confusing to me, you revised it to make your writing make sense. But know what? You didn't need me to say, 'I don't really get it' or 'Will you explain this?' You can reread your own story and find places where your story is confusing! I am going to go now. You have three more pages in your story. Would you reread each page all by yourself and find at least one more place on each page where readers could be confused? Then fix up one place on each page. Okay?"

Although I make it clear that I hadn't gleaned this from Alexa's text alone, I don't immediately tell Alexa she needs to add that information to the page. I'm hoping she'll intuit this and I want to leave her the space to do so.

One of the most important moves we make in a conference with a young writer is we wait. We wait far longer than seems normal. This wait time gives children a chance to self-initiate and to be active.

I don't believe that Alexa has totally gotten the hang of rereading her own writing and spotting the confusing sections. It is too early for me to even dream of saying, "Do this always when you write." For now, I am glad if she continues doing this work right now when I move on to another child.

PROCESS AND GOALS CONFERENCE
METHODS: Demonstration, Guided Practice

Teach the child to show, not tell.

Research

Observe, interview and read the child's writing to understand what the child is trying to do as a writer and student of revision. In this case, the child is revising by adding more detailed information onto the first page of her book.

I pulled a chair alongside Heather and watched as she reread her six-page booklet and began adding onto her first page. [*Fig. 5*]

"What a lucky time for you—making a strike!" I said. "In all my life, I have never made a strike. My ball always goes into the gutters."

Then, looking at Heather's draft, I said, "You are extra lucky. You not only made a strike; you also have a piece that truly deserves revision!"

Heather nodded, "I love this story," she said. "It's my best. I already revised. I put in 'It was at Chelsea Piers' 'cause I had to tell *where*."

Heather's story shows that she is taking early steps towards incorporating literary language into her text. If she were simply telling the story to a friend, she'd say, "I made a strike," instead of writing, "Once, at my birthday party, I made a strike." Her lead, especially, sounds like book language. The story is also structured like a narrative, complete with tension.

 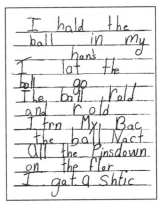

Fig. 5 Heather

Once at my birthday party I made a strike.
I held the ball in my hands.
I let the ball go.
The ball rolled and rolled. I turned my back.
The ball knocked all the pins down on the floor.
I got a strike.

Notice the unspoken assumption that only the best texts merit revision.

Name what the child has done as a writer. Remind her to do these things often in future writing.

"You are doing something really smart, you are showing *the setting* for the bowling party, showing *where your story took place*. That's smart work. Remember in *My Father's Dragon*, how we learned that the story was set on an island? Now you have added the setting to *your* story—just like in *My Father's Dragon*! Readers like to know where a story takes place. *Whenever* you write a story, do like you did today and think, 'Did I show my setting?'"

Probe to glean more about the child's intentions.

"After you add your setting, how will revise this story? Because you are right, it deserves revision," I said.

Heather was quiet, looking at the page. "I could say that we had chocolate cake and presents? And tell about the presents?" she suggested.

Decide/Teach

Weigh whether you want to accept or alter the child's intentions. In this case, you decide to teach by demonstrating how writers ask, "What am I trying to show in my story?" and "Which section of my story shows that?"

We can influence tomorrow's work not only by teaching children new strategies and goals, but also by noticing what they have already done that works and complimenting them on it. This is especially true for young children because often their best work happens almost by lucky coincidence. When we see and name what they have already done, we can help children to do this same thing again and to do it with deliberateness. Because my goal is to teach towards tomorrow, I don't say, "I love that you told readers that the bowling party was at Chelsea Piers." Instead I say, "I love that you added a setting."

When Heather starts telling me that she wants to add details about the birthday, alarms sound in my brain. Of course, Heather thinks of adding more details about the birthday, despite the fact that the birthday was entirely peripheral in this account of how she made a strike while bowling. I should have anticipated as much. I know, however, that if she does add a lot of information about the birthday, Heather's tightly focused Small Moment narrative will lose all its shapeliness. Yet, is it really possible for a six-year-old to discern relevant from irrelevant details? In the end, I figure Heather will have lots of chances to revise on her own, but for now, because I am on hand, I try to show her that writers revise to highlight what they decide is essential.

"You *could* tell about the birthday, the cake, the presents and all," I said, echoing the plans Heather had articulated. As I restated this option, my hand gestured that she could go on and on along that less-than-ideal vein. "But Heather, let me show you what I do when I revise. I do this." I took hold of her piece and acted as if I was the writer, musing aloud, "Let me think, what is this piece mainly about? If it becomes a book in the library, and kids pick it up to read it, what will they find that it is mainly about?"

Help the child get started doing what you have just demonstrated. Take the writer back to the beginning of the process you have demonstrated and help her reread her own writing, asking herself "What's this mainly about?"

Then, stepping out of role, I handed Heather her story and said, "Try it. Reread this and ask yourself, 'What is this piece mainly about?'"

Heather's eyes flickered over a page or two of her book. As she looked at the page, I asked her to ask the question to herself, "What's this book mainly about?" Then she announced, "It's about how I got a strike, but I didn't think I'd do good because I don't know how to bowl."

"I love the way you asked that question! 'What's it mainly about?' So it's about how you went bowling and you didn't think you'd do well because you didn't know how to bowl, and you worried, but then, lo and behold, you end up getting a strike!" I said. "Now, Heather, you need to ask a second question. You need to ask, 'Which section of the book shows the main idea of the story?' Because that's what you need to add onto."

Continue to demonstrate, and then help the child follow your lead.

"So Heather, let me show you what I do next. I reread and ask, 'Which section of this book shows my main idea, shows that I'm worried I won't do well because I don't know how to bowl.'" As I spoke, my eyes flickered over page one, page two. . . ." Will you reread and ask that?"

There are lots of possible teaching methods, and, in this instance, I choose to demonstrate. What this means is that I reenact, in a blow-by-blow fashion, what it is I want Heather to do. To make my demonstrations as helpful as possible, I think aloud so that Heather can peek in on the sorts of thoughts I hope she will have. I demonstrate a very tiny action, then ask Heather to try what I just did.

After I demonstrate a start-to-finish process that involves rereading and asking oneself a question, I need to take Heather back to the first step and set her up to start there.

Heather has just summarized her writing in ways that suggest it could become a much more poignant story, complete with tension and resolution. But the plot that she has just summarized still needs to be translated into story language and told in a sequential, blow-by-blow fashion. Heather could do that work on her own, but the teaching point I'm making in this conference is complex enough already, so I give Heather a hand by repeating her story back to her in a way that makes it a sequential narrative. This is a very supportive move.

I passed the book (and the role) to Heather, who began to reread the birthday page. I nudged her to repeat the question. She did, then said, "Not this page 'cause it's about the birthday."

"Point to a place where you think you could add more that does go with the main thing that your story is about."

Heather reread the book, and quickly pointed to the page where she had written, "I held the ball in my hands. I let the ball go."

Link

Name what the child has done as a writer, and remind her to do this often in future writing. Set her up to continue working.

Then I added, "Heather, when I want to add more onto one part of my story, I do just what you have done. I reread my story and think, 'What is my piece mainly about?' and 'Where could I say more to really build up the main thing in my writing?' Now you have done the same thing I do! From now on, whenever you want to revise, start by rereading and asking, 'What is this mainly about?'"

* * *

Notice and Switch to a Second Process Conference

"So Heather, I know you know how to reread and add on. Do that on this page."

Heather reread the page and picked up her pencil. "Here, I am going to say, 'I was worried because I didn't know how to bowl,'" she said.

I have just taught Heather two questions she needs to ask often. First, I taught her to ask, "What am I trying to show in my story?" and then I taught her to ask, "Which section shows that?" By now, it is fairly obvious that she shouldn't add more about the birthday, but I let her make this decision and articulate the rationale. When I ask her to point to the place in her text where she might add more that "goes with" the main thing in this story, she can do this easily. I'm trying to set her up to be active and to make a string of good decisions. With my support, Heather rereads her draft and thinks, "What section needs to be developed more to convey what I want to convey?"

There are lots of intersections in a conference where we need to decide if we have taught enough already or if we want to try to take the child up one more step. I could easily have left this conference as it was and considered it an effective conference. I've taught plenty for today. I decide, however, that I want Heather to do some work that could become an exemplar for the class and, for that reason, I press on with one more teaching point.

Research/Decide/Teach

Weigh whether you want to accept or alter the child's intentions. In this case, you decide to make a second teaching point, teaching the child that when a writer wants to add her feelings into a story, the writer tries to *show* how she felt rather than explicitly telling the feeling. Teach by giving the child guided practice in reenacting her story to recall details she can use to "show, not tell."

"Heather, you are right that you could just tell the reader, 'I was worried because I didn't know how to bowl.' But earlier in the year we learned that writers have a saying. It is this: 'show, not tell.' Could I help you to instead *show* your reader that you were new to bowling and worried about how you'd do?" Heather nodded that she was game for this.

Help the child get started doing what you hope she will do.

I proceeded. "Right now, can you act out how you started bowling? Try to remember exactly what you were doing and thinking."

Interject lean, efficient prompts to scaffold the child's reenactment in a step-by-step fashion.

"So get up and pretend you were at the bowling alley. Show me what you did and say what you thought."

Heather clambered to her feet and assumed bowling position. "See, I held the ball in my hands," she said, and held an imaginary ball.

Furiously scribing a transcript of what Heather said, I prompted, "What did you think?"

"I thought it would go in the gutters."

"Keep going. Act out what you did next," I prompted, continuing to transcribe what she said.

"I let the ball go." Heather said, reenacting in slow motion the way she released the ball.

Interject lean prompts to lift the level of what the child is doing.

"Say exactly what you did."

"My arm went down and my, my, waist went down," she said, as she reenacted the position bowlers take as they release the ball. "Then I looked away 'cause I didn't want to see it," she said, referring to the fact that she

---

Notice that I first tell Heather my intentions, then I get her started doing something. This is very much like the rhythm in a minilesson when we always explain what we're after before launching into an example.

I often ask children to make a movie in their minds of themselves, doing the thing they want to describe on the page. This is just a more concrete version of the same thing.

Children learn mental actions through physical ones. By asking Heather to physically re-enact the vignette she is trying to capture on paper, I'm showing her the mental processes behind any frequent urging to "make a movie of what you did in your mind and then write it down, bit by bit."

didn't want to see the ball roll into the gutters.

"And then?" I prompted.

"Then I saw it and I said, 'I got a strike!' 'I got a strike!'" Heather said, reenacting how she jumped for glee.

Take the child back to the beginning of what you have elicited through guided practice and help her get started putting this on the page.

"So Heather, will you reread this first page and ask yourself, 'Is there anything I should add on here that shows the exact story of what happened when you went bowling, and how you worried and all? Do you need to add more onto this page?" I asked, opening her book to the page we'd discussed at some length.

Predictably, Heather said, "No, 'cause my book isn't mainly about the birthday party."

"Would you reread the next page," I opened to the page about holding the ball, "and think if there is more you can add? Remember what you said as you acted this out," and I reread my transcript of what she'd said earlier. Soon Heather had added to this page and the next:

> I held the ball in my hands. *It was heavy. I thought it would go down the gutters.*
> I let the ball go. *My arm went down, my waist went down.*

Link

Name what the child has done as a writer, and remind her to do this often in the future. Set her up to continue working.

"I love the way you reread your story, decided on the main part, then added more to build up that part. It really helped you to act out the moment and remember details. I hope you do this often when you write and revise. Keep going on the remaining pages for now." I said, and left.

Later, I found Heather had continued revising. This is her completed revised book. [*Fig. 6*]

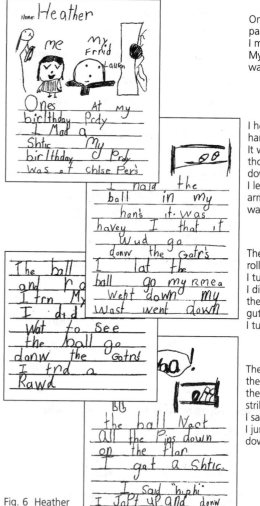

I keep asking Heather to say why she wouldn't add on the somewhat irrelevant part. I do this because I want to reinforce what Heather has learned, and this is the portion of today's conference that I think stands the best chance of becoming part of Heather's ongoing repertoire. I know that, for now, a good portion of this conference is still new and complicated for Heather and that she'd require my presence if she wanted to do similar work with another text.

Once at my birthday party
I made a strike.
My birthday party was at Chelsea Piers.

I held the ball in my hands.
It was heavy. I thought it would go down the gutters.
I let the ball go. My arm went down, my waist went down.

The ball rolled and rolled.
I turned my back.
I did not want to see the ball go down the gutters.
I turned around.

The ball knocked all the pins down on the floor. I got a strike.
I said "yippee."
I jumped up and down.

Fig. 6 Heather

PROCESS AND GOALS CONFERENCE
METHOD: Guided Practice

Teach a child to revise by adding descriptive details.

Research

Observe and interview to understand what the child is trying to do as a writer and as a student of revision. In this case, the child knows he is expected to revise but is unsure how to begin.

At the end of the minilesson, I asked children to begin their revision by rereading their pieces, and Larry did this willingly. But then, when he reached the end of his piece, he just looked blankly at the final page. He picked up a pen and began to darken in the letters "The End."

"Hi, Larry," I said, drawing my chair in close. "I watched you reread that book of yours. What ideas did you come up with for revising it?"

Larry looked at me a bit blankly.

I tried again, "What are your plans for revision today?" I asked.

"The one about getting new shoes," Larry answered and waited for me to say something.

I was quiet, hoping he'd say more. The silence was palpable.

Finally, Larry added, "I don't know what to add."

"Can you read me the part of your story you might want to revise?" I prompted, and Larry read his first three pages to me. See Figure 7 on page 49.

Notice that I persevere in my effort to get Larry to name what he's trying to do as a writer.

This is still research. I'm trying to understand Larry's intentions and having trouble getting him to articulate them to me. As I see Larry struggle with my inquiries, I shift gears so that my questions and prompts demand less and less of him. However, I don't take over and tell him what to do. The request for him to read me the section of his draft that he wants to revise allows Larry to read aloud a chosen section of his text and, in doing so, teach me what he has in mind for his writing.

I looked at the store.
I ran in to the store. Zoom!
I looked around the store.

Name what the child has already done, and remind him to do this often in the future.

"Larry, I love that you have a whole book just about buying sneakers. I hope that for the rest of your life, you remember that it really works for you when you write about tiny, focused events. Who would have thought there'd be a whole book just on buying sneakers! That is really smart. And I definitely agree that this book is worthy of revision. It is also smart to decide that you want to fix up your lead; the beginning of a book matters a lot."

Probe to glean more about the child's intentions.

"So, how do you think you could make your lead even better?"

"I dunno, really," Larry answered.

"Well, how *might* you change it? What *could* you do?"

"Add on?"

Decide/Teach

Weigh whether you want to accept or alter the child's intentions or to generate others. In this case, you decide to teach the child that writers often study an exemplar text to get ideas for improving writing. Explicitly tell him what you expect he will do next (and often) when he writes, and then give him guided practice looking at and learning from another text, then applying what he admires to his own writing.

"One thing I do sometimes is I look at other authors who've done the sort of writing I want to do. We could maybe look back at *A Chair for My Mother* and notice Vera's part about the store, because you and she are both writing about stores." I opened the book and began to read, "'We shopped through four furniture stores. We tried out big chairs and smaller ones, high chairs and low chairs. . . .' What do you notice?"

"She is, like, telling about big and small and high up chairs. Telling stuff about the store."

I suspect Larry hasn't chosen this section carefully. When I'd asked him to reread a section, he'd grabbed the first section that met his eye. Nevertheless, I decide to act as if Larry has deliberately chosen to revise his lead.

Early in the conference, I find it helpful to try to see what the child has already done and to make sure the child does this again. In this conference, for example, my first instinct is to think about Larry's resistance and his passivity. But the fact that I have an empty slot in my internalized conference outline that is called "name what the child has already done" nudges me to cast another glance over Larry's work and, this time, to see a good deal that merits celebration.

Notice that my research is fairly prolonged. I don't rush to conclude that this child has no real intentions for revision.

Larry hasn't given me very clear direction over what he wants to do with his piece. I'm assuming some of the control here by asking him to look between a page of A Chair for My Mother *and his book, but I still insist on him being the one to notice something Vera Williams did that he could emulate. I'm helping him get a direction for his writing.*

I don't pump too many detailed observations out of him because I want Larry to see that he can do a lot with whatever he notices.

"You are right! She does tell a lot of detailed information, doesn't she?" I said as if I'd never before noticed this. "Larry, when you study another author's book, it is like that author is giving you tips on your writing. It's like Vera is saying, 'Larry, *you* might try telling a lot of information in *your* book.' Do you think you want take Vera Williams' advice and describe more, tell a lot of information about the sneaker store?"

Larry nodded his head. But he still had a blank stare on his face. I was not sure if he truly understood what I had just taught him.

Help the child get started doing what you hope he will do. In this instance, help him recall the story. Then say and write more details about it.

"I bet Vera sat at her desk and remembered that chair store. Can you do that? Can you remember and describe the Sketchers store?"

"It was the biggest Sketchers I ever saw. It looked like a basement." Larry replied.

"Those details really help me picture it!" I said. "Why don't you add those details to your story?" Pointing to his first page, I dictated back what he'd said to me. "Right here, you could add, 'It was the biggest Sketchers I ever saw.' Then you can read the next page like we just did, and think, "What could I add on here . . . and so forth."

Larry picked up his pen and began to write. The first three pages turned into what's shown in Figure 6.

Link

Name (and get the child to name) what he has done as a writer, and remind him to do this often in the future.

"So Larry, you've done some amazing revisions."

"Remember at the start of our conference, you weren't sure how to get started revising. What strategy did you use today to get started revising?"

"Um, I showed the store."

I act as if I'm merely saying back what Larry has just said, but in fact I extrapolate for him some qualities of good writing that are found in the sections of Vera Williams' text that he spotlights. The quality of good writing can't be "tell about the kind of furniture in the store" because that isn't exportable to a great many pieces!

I looked at the store. It was the biggest Sketchers I ever saw and I wondered what did that s stand for. I ran in to the store so fast. "I just could not wait" I said and I kicked the door open.

I looked around the store, it looked like a basement with shoes, but I recognized that it actually looked like Sketchers because there were a lot of people and shelves.

Fig. 7 Larry

I am nudging Larry to do this work of extrapolating the exportable lesson.

"Yes. But the first thing you did was that you read a book you really liked, and you thought, 'What did this author do that I might want to try?' That is a really smart revision strategy, and you'll want to use that strategy often if you aren't sure how to revise. Smart work!"

When you are asking the children to name what they are doing, this can act like a form of assessment. If they describe what they are doing, they probably understand it reasonably well. If not, this may be an indication that this child (or the whole class) needs more work in this area.

PART FIVE

AUTHORS AS MENTORS

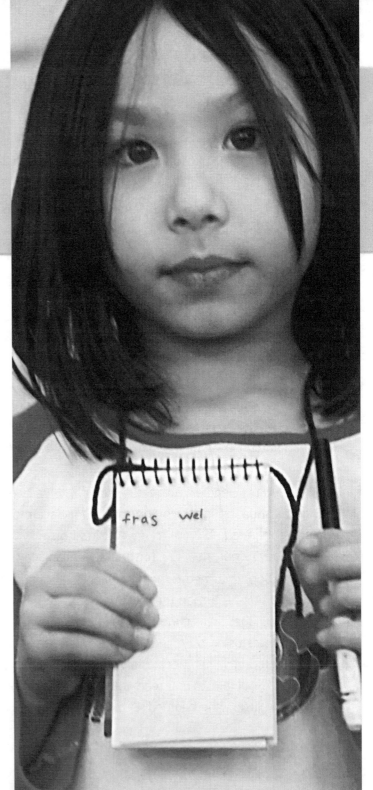

This is an ambitious unit, and you'll need to closely align your conferences with your minilessons. Become accustomed to reading the minilesson ahead of time and thinking, "What will my work be in conferences today?"

At the start, this unit will feel like the Small Moments unit, but it has been a while since your children generated focused, sequential Small Moment stories. Your children will need to be reminded to zoom in on a small vignette, envision it, say the story aloud prior to writing it, and so forth. Reread the Small Moments conferences to prepare yourself for the start of this unit, only, because of your new author-study angles, you'll want to rely on your mentor author to help you teach the importance of focus, detail, chronological sequence, and the like. You'll say things like, "I'll bet that when Ezra Jack Keats went to write this book, the first thing he did was. . . ."

Soon your agenda in conferences will switch. Now you'll want to help children study exemplar texts, noticing what the author has done as a writer and speculating why the author might have used this technique. Your conferences will sometimes feel like reading conferences. That's okay. Teach kids to read texts like craftspeople, noticing another person's writing decisions. Don't manipulate children into seeing and saying what you have in mind; the goal is for the children to be able to admire the craft in another writer's work and to emulate that craft. "Why don't you try that?" you'll say to almost anything that the children notice. Now this unit will feel a bit like the Revision unit of study, as the writer applies a quality of good writing to his or her draft.

Finally, you may want to teach children that authors don't always write Small Moment stories, and to use your class author study and children's own author studies to open new possibilities. Throughout the upcoming conferences, pay special attention to the methods we use to teach.

PROCESS AND GOALS CONFERENCE
METHODS: Explicitly Tell, Guided Practice

Help a child learn more about punctuation from studying the text of a mentor author.

Research

Observe, interview, and read the child's writing to understand what the child is trying to do as a writer and as a participant in an author study. In this case, the child has emulated an author by adding ellipses, which she hopes alters the pace of her writing.

Sophia was busy adding more windows to the picture she had drawn of her car. She was concentrating, her tongue stuck out a little bit. I watched for a minute, then approached.

"Sophia! What are you working on as a writer today?"

"I finished the writing part of my story and now I am going back to add details. I am putting in windows for my car because there are four windows in my car!"

It was not the right time for a discussion on perspective or counting, so I nodded my head and waited to see if Sophia had more to say. It was unusual to find a situation in which Sophia did *not* have more to say! After a slight pause, she continued, "I went to my cousin's house for Christmas last year. I'm Jewish but they're *not*, they're Christmas. You can see them!"

Sophia turned to her last page to show me the beaming people she had drawn. As she turned the pages, I noticed that she had included ellipses on the second page. I was curious to see how she was using them, because I'd seen her classmates using them in a host of different ways. But meanwhile I also wondered how her piece as a whole went.

"Sophia, can you read your whole piece to me from the beginning?"

"Sure," she beamed. She read. [*Fig. 8*]

It's a good thing for a writer to return to a finished piece to add details so the writer's text matches her mental image. You will probably not be content with revisions that affect the illustrations only, but you should still feel pleased when children self-initiate these revisions.

Sophia's cousins are probably Christians rather than Christmases, but it isn't necessary for me to correct Sophia on every little thing. I am trying to determine the main gist of this writer's intention.

I don't point this out to Sophia, but I wondered why she'd focused on the car ride, rather than the visit. Was the car ride the heart of her story or had she simply begun at the start of the trip and then added details because she'd been taught to do so, resulting in details of a car ride? I figured another time I might remind her to ask herself, before she starts to write, "What's the most important thing I am trying to say about my topic?" For now, I set aside these questions.

Fig. 8   Sophia

I love when I go to my cousins' on Christmas.
Last year I was in the car. I . . . was waiting and waiting and waiting.
So finally we were there. I pushed open the door and dashed in the front door.

Name what the child has already done, and remind her to do this often in future work.

"Sophia, I love how you wrote that you 'dashed' in the door—I can picture in my mind how you went in really quickly! You could have just said 'I *went* inside,' but you found the exactly true word that really showed *how* excited you were to get there! Using the *exactly true* action words is a real talent."

Probe to glean more about the child's intentions.

"I noticed something else, too—here on the second page—can you tell me a little bit about these?" I pointed to the ellipses that she used incorrectly.

"Oh, that's ellipses to make you slow down when you read it."

Stephen Covey, *author of* Seven Habits of Highly Effective People, *suggests that parents are wise to catch their child in the act of doing something good and to praise that behavior. The same is true for teachers of writing. It's important to praise in ways that teach a larger principle. Notice, here, that I don't settle for telling Sophia that* dashed *is a good word—instead I try to support her in using precise action words.*

"Cool! Can you say more about why you put those in right there, after *I*?"

"Well it's because I was waiting and waiting in the car to get to my cousins' house, and I put them there so it would show a long time of waiting."

Don't assume that the child's first response is all the child has to say. Pursue the response a bit.

By zeroing in on Sophia's use of ellipses, I am taking lead in this conference and steering it towards the subject of reading-writing connections. Although I choose the subject of our discussion, I know she needs to inform me on the ideas that guide her. Remember not to assume you know the logic that guided a child. Ask!

"That is such a great reason to use ellipses! You are right that ellipses slow a piece down. You were being just like Angela Johnson when you had the idea to do that."

Decide/Teach

Weigh whether you want to accept or alter the child's intentions. In this case, you decide to teach the child more about ellipses and about learning from another author. Teach by explicitly telling the child more about ellipses and by giving the child guided practice studying another author's text.

"Sophia, I want to teach you one more thing about ellipses. When writers use ellipses, they put them *exactly in the place* where they want readers to slow themselves down. Where in your text do you want your readers to slow down?"

"Well, at the waiting part!"

"I thought so—see how your ellipses are right after this word *I* though? That makes us slow our reading down on *I* and not at the waiting part. So I'd read your sentence like this, 'I . . . (long pause) was waiting and waiting and waiting.'"

Help the child get started doing what you hope she will do.

"I was noticing that Liam was using ellipses in his work today too, and I think maybe he can help us out here." Liam, who sat across the table from Sophia, had been working on a piece about when his mommy was in Los Angeles. In his story, he said he was waiting for his mother to get back and give him a Kobe Bryant basketball shirt. He had placed ellipses appropriately (and also used them to elongate the waiting), so that one sentence read, "I wait . . . wait . . . wait . . . and then my Mommy brought me my Bryant shirt."

"Liam, may Sophia and I learn from you right now? I was noticing that you were using ellipses in your piece about waiting for your mom to bring you your Bryant shirt. Can you read that part to us?"

Liam obligingly read his sentence. Speaking to Sophia, I said, "What do you notice about the way Liam used the ellipses?"

"He put them here." Sophia pointed to the word *wait*."

Sophia has used ellipses in an odd fashion. ("Last year I was in the car. I . . . was waiting and waiting and waiting.") Often when a child is partly wrong, the child is also partly correct. Sophia was wise to use ellipses in the first place and to associate them with slowing down, and in these ways her incorrect use of ellipses was partly right. I admire what she's done that is right.

In our minilessons, we try to explicitly name what we are trying to teach. It's helpful to do the same in conferences.

Remember, it said, "Last year I was in the car. I . . . [was] waiting and waiting and waiting."

It's nice to sometimes have children learn from exemplary writing by other children. You'll see that later I make a passing reference to "writers like you and Liam and Angela Johnson." These asides make a world of difference.

Notice that I ask Sophia to use the same steps to learn from Liam's writing that she and other students also use to learn from Angela Johnson's writing. In both instances, I ask the children to name what the mentor author has done that they admire.

Interject lean, efficient prompts to raise the level of what the child is doing.

"I wonder why?"

"Because he wants you to slow down."

"Can you read his page, the way he wrote it?"

"I wait . . . wait . . . wait . . . and then my Mommy brought me my Bryant shirt."

"So you're thinking he put the ellipses right after the word *wait*, because that's where he wanted us, readers, to slow down? That's what writers like you and Liam and Angela Johnson do when you use ellipses—you put them right at the exact part where you want readers to be silent and to slow down. Waiting *is* slow isn't it?"

Sophia nodded. "It is. It's like forever."

"And that is what you want your reader to feel? Where do you think you could put *your* ellipses so that they make sense?"

Sophia reread her sentence: "I was waiting and waiting and waiting." Then she said, "I could put them after this *waiting*, and I could put them again after this *waiting*, too."

Link

Name what the child has done as a writer, and remind her to do this often in future writing.

"Great idea! But the bigger lesson is that whenever you are working on your writing, you can take a text where the author has done something you want to try, and then you can study it closely and try to do the same thing. I'm going to leave you a book that has another bit of really cool punctuation. I've put a sticky note on the one page I hope you'll study," I said and gave her *Fireflies* by Julie Brinckloe. "When you finish what you are working on, would you see if you can figure out how the new punctuation I'm leaving you 'wants' to be read and see if you can add similar punctuation into one of your stories? Would you be willing to try that? You're going to be our class expert on punctuation!"

Notice that I try to have Sophia do most of the work. Instead of pointing out what I notice about Liam's text, I get her to extrapolate an observation and to reach for an explanation for why Liam may have done this. I also ask her to read aloud Liam's text in a way that reflects his use of ellipses. The conference would be faster if I did all this, saying, "Notice that Liam did such and such. He did it for such and such reason," but children learn more from what they do than from what we do. I especially want Sophia to be active right here at this point in the conference because what I'm trying to teach is not really ellipses. I am trying to show her how she can study and learn from a mentor text. It's important, therefore, that she's doing this work in our conference.

I could have brought the conference to a close without this added challenge, but my sense was that Sophia would be eager to be pushed and that she enjoys playing with tempo and intonation in her own writing. Why not seize the moment to nudge her even farther!

PROCESS AND GOALS CONFERENCE
METHOD: Guided Practice

Teach a child to emulate whatever she admires in another author's text.

Research

Observe, interview, and read the child's writing to learn what the child is trying to do as a participant in an author study. In this case, the child is adding a sentence that conveys a more detailed description onto each page of her book.

Amanda watched from a distance, as Joline busily taped a strip of paper onto the edge of her draft so that after the sentence, "I first saw a Milky Way," Joline had now written, "It was looking like ice."

Amanda approached Joline, "What are you working on as a writer today, Joline?"

"I'm revising," she said with enthusiasm. "I put in more detail about what the Milky Way looked like!"

As the year unfurls, one of the biggest differences you will notice in the conferences is that the work children do before the conference begins will change. In Small Moments, almost every conference began with a child adding color to her pictures. In this unit of study, even before we begin a conference, writers will often be revising and rethinking their writing.

Name what the child has already done as a writer, and remind her to do this often in future writing.

"I am glad you are revising *and* that the new part really helps readers picture what you are describing. Because if you had left it, 'I saw the Milky Way, I saw (whatever else),' I'd feel badly because *you* got to see those and we, your readers, didn't. This detail really gets me started seeing that Milky Way in *my* mind. Who knows? You may even make bigger flaps and add in even more description to help me see that Milky Way!"

You'll be amazed at the power of sentences like the last two: "Who knows? You may even make bigger flaps and add in even more. . . ."

Probe to glean more about the child's intentions.

"Joline, can you read the whole story to me, from the beginning?" Amanda knew from previous conferences that an earlier version of Joline's piece had been structured like a list, and wondered whether that had changed.

"I looked up," Joline read from the first page. "I first saw a Milky Way. It looked like ice." Then she read, "I saw Jupiter. It was gold." Then, "I saw the moon in the sky," and finally, "And I went home."

"What's your plan, Joline? What will you do next?"

"Add on more about the moon."

"Oh! So every page will first tell the big thing you saw—the Milky Way, Jupiter, the moon—and then every page will tell what you noticed about what you saw? 'It looked like ice . . . It was gold. . . .' What a nice pattern!"

Joline nodded. "The next page already has what I saw and what it looked like, but I didn't say it the best."

"That's smart of you to realize. So will you fix it up?"

Joline nodded again. "I know how!"

Decide/Teach

Weigh whether you want to accept or alter the child's intentions. In this case, you decide to teach the child how to look at a mentor text to learn more ways to fancy up her list-like description of the sky. Teach by providing her with guided practice in searching for a text that is similar to hers and then inquiring about what techniques that text's author has used to fancy it up. In this instance, the child notices the text's repeating refrain. Help the writer get started doing what you hope she will do. In this case, help the child choose a mentor text.

"I want to show you another thing you can do as you revise, Joline. When I try to improve my writing, I think, 'Do I know any books that are sort of like the one I'm writing?'"

Notice that Amanda has looked over the whole expanse of Joline's writing and seen a pattern emerge and she asks, as if naively, whether Joline intends to continue writing in this pattern. Chances are good Joline wasn't aware of the pattern before Amanda brought it into her consciousness. If we can recognize and name the big picture of what a child has done, this is very helpful. It's worthwhile for teachers to practice doing this.

Amanda has decisions to make. Joline's story could use help. Joline knows this and so she's adding descriptive details—a reasonable effort to improve the text. Amanda could go with this direction, encouraging Joline to continue adding detail or to add a repeating refrain to unify her story, and so on. Alternatively, Amanda could help Joline see that "her story" is really not a story because nothing happens to the main character. There is no tension or resolution in this "story," and the character doesn't undergo a transformation. If Amanda asks, "What's the story really about?" or "Why'd you decide to write this?" she will probably help the writer realize that there may have been a before and after implicit in the text (that is, "Before I thought the sky was boring but then I saw . . . and I realized . . ." or "It had been a lousy day. But then I looked into the night sky . . . and my day was changed."). Amanda decides, however, to go with Joline's intention. Amanda plans to help Joline dress up her list-like book by making small improvements on it.

"Your book contains a list of all the things you saw in the night sky. I'm trying to think if I know any famous books that are like yours—that list all the things the narrator sees or does and tells a little about each. Um . . . um . . ."

"Do Like Kyla!"

"Yes! Because in your book, Joline, on each page, you tell what you see and give some details about it. And on each page in *Do Like Kyla*, Angela tells how the little sister is like Kyla and gives some details about that. They books are structured practically the same!"

Help the writer get started doing what you hope she will do. In this case, help her study the mentor text and look for ideas about how to fancy up her own piece.

"Let's look at a page or two of *Do Like Kyla* (that's what I do, I study texts that are practically the same as mine) and see if we get any ideas for other ways to fix up *The Night Sky*." Soon Amanda and Joline were poring over an excerpt for *Do Like Kyla*.

> Mama says, "Lots of sunshine today."
> Kyla kisses the sunbeam on the dog's head.
> I do like Kyla.
> We're going to the store so Kyla helps me put my coat on.
> "Warm now," she says.
> I do like Kyla and say, "Warm now."

Joline interrupted, "She uses a comeback line! 'I do like Kyla.' Just like in *Joshua's Night Whispers*!"

It would be easy to simply direct Joline's attention to a book, but our rule of thumb in a conference is that we try to remember we are teaching the writer, not the writing. If the writing gets better but the writer hasn't learned a strategy she can use another day with another text, we have wasted our time. Amanda needs to be sure that Joline is especially active in the sections of this conference in which she introduces the strategies that she suggests will work for her another time. In this instance, Amanda hopes to teach Joline to search for an author who has done something rather like what she is trying to do, and so Amanda needs her to be actively involved in this.

When you encourage children to make reading-writing connections, go to the actual text you are learning from and study a bit of it. Don't learn from your general memory of it alone. Let the child do the work—noticing whatever she notices—and be prepared to be surprised by what she sees.

Although Amanda would welcome a surprising observation, she already knew that chances were good that Joline would notice the use of a comeback line in this excerpt.

Interject lean prompts to lift the level of what the child is doing.

"You're right. Angela Johnson keeps saying, 'I do like Kyla.' Hmmm. I wonder how she picked *that* line?"

"'Cause it's the main thing in her story. I can do that."

"So you want to add a comeback line, Joline? What is the part you want to repeat?" Amanda asked.

"Umm, well . . . my story is about when I looked up into the sky. . . ."

"So it's about when you looked up? What do you think the repeating line could be that might show that?"

"I could repeat, 'when I looked up'?"

Take the child back to the beginning of what you elicited through guided practice and help her get started putting this on the page.

"Okay!" Amanda said. "Let's write your refrain on slips of paper and then you can reread what you've written and decide where you want to add that particular refrain or a different one." As Amanda spoke, she filled three sentence strips with the phrase and handed each to Joline, "We'll tape it on."

Joline flipped to the first page, and looked up at Amanda. "Could I put 'when I looked up' right before I saw the Milky Way?"

"Okay," Amanda nodded, saying as little as possible.

Laying a second sentence strip on another page, Joline said, "And this one goes before, 'I saw Jupiter'?" Amanda nodded.

Link

Name what the child has done as a writer, and remind her to do this often in future writing. Set her up to continue working.

Joline taped the sentence strip on and began rereading the upcoming section of her text, a third sentence strip in hand.

"You're being just like Angela Johnson. So you are going to finish borrowing Angela Johnson's use of comeback lines and then you are going to continue adding detail—and you've already done that on your first page. Great work!"

Of course Amanda doesn't really wonder why Angela Johnson picked her refrain. Often when we want to engage a child in a line of thinking, instead of directing the child to answer our question, we think aloud in a way that recruits the child to join us in mulling over a question. There is another example of this earlier in this conference when Amanda muses, "I'm trying to think if I know any famous books that are like yours."

Amanda is dying for Joline to choose a better phrase, but this is not Amanda's story, it is Joline's, and Amanda guards herself against usurping control.

It can be enormously helpful if you can make the technical, logistical details easier as Amanda does for Joline in this instance.

It's wise to remind Joline that she has another agenda—adding descriptive details—as well as the sentence strip project.

PROCESS AND GOALS CONFERENCE
METHODS: Guided Practice, Assessment Practice

Teach a child to notice more aspects of a mentor author's writing.

Research

Observe, interview, and read the child's writing to understand what the child is trying to do as a participant in an author study. In this case, the child is using a mentor text to help him improve the quality of writing in his draft.

I watched Sudhir bent over his paper, writing as if no one else was in the room.

"Sudhir, may I interrupt?" I asked softly, kneeling down beside him.

He sat up straight, bristling with pride. "I'm writing about my belt test in Tae Kwon Do!" Sudhir had been writing about Tae Kwon Do for several days—the topic seemed to be a great source of inspiration for him, and he had a lot to say about it.

"I'm to the end part where I got my high yellow belt and I was so proud."

"You look proud even talking about it, Sudhir! May I look at your piece?" [*Fig. 9*]

Probe to glean more about the child's intentions.

"So Sudhir, now I've read your story. Can you tell me more exactly what you are working on as a writer?"

It was Thursday morning. Suddenly I woke up. "It's my belt test!" I shouted very loudly as I jumped on my bed. Then my mom came into my room. She asked me what's so exciting? "My belt test! My belt test!"

it Was thursday Morning sodintly I woke up "its my Bilt tist!" I Shoutid Very Lawdly as I JoMpt oN My bRd then My MoM CaMe iN My RooM She asct Me Wats so exiting? My BiLt tist My BiLt tist

I was so proud of myself. I was going to get my high yellow belt in Tae Kwon Do!

I Vasso pRoud of My Silf IWas going tn get My Hie Ylloc Bilt in tikVondo

Fig. 9   Sudhir

It is faster when we read their writing, and so very often we do this.

By now I know the content of Sudhir's writing and I have lots of ideas for what I'd do if this was my story. But, of course, it's not my story, and I need to know more about Sudhir's plans and intentions before I can teach him. I discipline myself to probe and listen more before seizing on a particular line of work.

"I read *Koala Lou* and she has a contest like I do and Mem Fox really shows that the tree climbing contest was exciting and I'm doing that same thing. I added this (an exclamation point) and I am going to say, 'I was really REALLY excited!'"

Name what the child has already done as a writer and remind him to do this often in future writing.

"You've done a smart thing. You saw which part of Mem Fox's writing could especially help you. You noticed that when she described the gum tree climbing contest, she wrote in a way that showed how exciting the contest was and now you, too, want to show excitement. I love the way you focused on one page of Mem's work and asked, 'What *exactly* has she done that can teach me?'"

Decide/Teach

Weigh whether you want to accept or alter the child's intentions. In this case, you decide to help the child learn from the exemplar he's selected, noticing and emulating not only the exclamation point but also the way the author uses "show, not tell" to create a sense of excitement. Teach by providing the child with guided practice in how to study a mentor author's text.

"May I watch how you go about studying what Mem Fox has done? May we look at the page together?"

The two of us read and reread the chosen page. I was silent, hoping Sudhir would comment on what he noticed, and he did. "She tells that they waved their party hats."

"You are right. She doesn't just say, 'The spectators cheered,' she tells *exactly how* they cheered. 'The spectators whistled *and cheered and wildly waved their party hats.*"

Interject lean, efficient prompts to scaffold the child's work in a step-by-step fashion.

"Sudhir, let's name what Mem Fox did and see if she does that again, okay?" I paused to see if Sudhir would step in and do this but wasn't surprised when he didn't. "She used exact action words, didn't she? Let's see if she does that on her page," I said and turned to another page where she did do this.

It may seem like a miracle that, on his own initiative, this child has found a text to emulate and selected a section of that text that can inform his own text, but of course this isn't the result of magic but of carefully designed instruction. Every child in the room has practiced making reading-writing connections by emulating Angela Johnson's writing, and now each child has his own mentor author. More specifically, each child has selected a page or two in a mentor text that can inform his writing. Sudhir has noticed the obvious, identifying Mem Fox's use of exclamation marks and bold print to convey excitement. Sudhir's piece won't get a lot better merely by adding exclamation marks, but his writing will improve over time because he apprentices himself to mentor authors.

I always want to name what a child has done in a way that in fact lifts the level of the child's actions. It could well be that Sudhir selected the gum tree contest as an exemplar simply because Mem Fox and he both wrote about contests. I act as if he deliberately selected this passage because Mem, like Sudhir, wrote in a way that conveyed excitement, regardless of the actual reason.

It is important to notice that Mem Fox doesn't describe how the crowd cheered with a list of adverbs ("The crowd cheered loudly and wildly and happily") but instead adds very particular details about the spectators' party hats.

I set Sudhir up to do some successful work fairly easily, and then I name what he's done.

Soon Sudhir had pointed to a section of the text that described Koala Lou's climbing. "Say more," I prompted.

"Well," Sudhir said, "It doesn't just say that Koala Lou climbed, it says *how* she climbed. 'Higher and higher and faster and faster.' She is going up that tree really fast," Sudhir said.

"Let's look at your piece, Sudhir. Maybe you could use exact action words like Mem does to show *how* you do things? What are you doing on this first page?"

"I'm shouting."

"Okay," I said, and lightly touched the page where Mem Fox's spectators cheered by whistling and wildly waving their party hats. I'm hoping to nudge Sudhir to use Mem Fox as a model.

"I can say, 'I shouted really loud'?"

Interject lean prompts to lift the level of what the child is doing.

"*How* are you shouting?"

"Jumping up and down."

"Put it together, Sudhir. Say what you'll write on this page."

"I was shouting very loudly, and I was jumping on the bed, too!"

I said nothing and watched to see if Sudhir would continue doing more of this on his own. He continued, instead, to bask in his success, so I touched the next page of his book. "Come on. Keep going. There are other places where you can add *how* you did things. I'll come check on you after you work for a while."

Link

Name what the child has done as a writer, and remind him to do this often in future writing. Set him up to continue working.

Shortly after I left, I noticed Sudhir reread a line that had said, "I ran into class." He added on so it now said, "I ran rite in my class so quickly."

"Sudhir! You're being *just* like Mem Fox! Always remember that you can put an author's books beside your own and get so many ideas for improving your writing. Congratulations." Sudhir beamed.

Notice that my prompts are concise ones.

It is important that our prompts are as lean as possible. In this conference, the gesture of touching a page acts as a prompt, nudging Sudhir to do some work that he is quite ready to do.

Here I want to help Sudhir synthesize the details into sentences.

PART SIX

NONFICTION WRITING: PROCEDURES AND REPORTS

You'll want to draw on your entire repertoire of conferences in this unit. Because your children will move in sync through the process of writing one or two How-To texts and then an All-About text, you know that many children will be facing similar challenges on any one day. Early on, when children are just starting their How-to books and then later, when they are just starting their All-About books, your conferences will resemble those from the Small Moments unit, only this time you'll be setting children up to rehearse for—and then to plan and to write—non-narratives rather than narratives. Then, once the children have drafts-in-progress, your conferences will be rather like those you held during the Revision and Authors as Mentors units. You'll help children look at published texts and at an exemplar you write and use what they see to help them revise their first drafts. Finally, when you help children edit, your conferences will resemble those you did during the Writing for Readers unit.

You may find, however, that your conferences in this unit are different from the rest in two major ways. More often, now, you'll confer with two writers at a time, as in the first conference for this book. Here, Laurie intervenes to help one child function as a writing teacher for the other. Then, too, you'll put a new spotlight on the importance of writing for an audience. To some extent, then, your role will be to give writers a trial audience.

PROCESS AND GOALS CONFERENCE
METHOD: Demonstrate

Teach a child to reread for sense.

Research

Interview and observe to understand what the children are trying to do as writers and as students of nonfiction writing. In this case, the children are trying to ensure that their directions make sense.

When I pulled alongside Melissa and her partner Nicole, the girls were trying to figure out how to "try out" Melissa's directions for making chocolate lollipops. Melissa held the writing aloft as if she was the conductor of an orchestra that was now rebelling. Nicole had a pout on her face, and she threw up her hands with exasperation.

"So, writers, what are you doing as writers today?"

Nicole said, "I am supposed to try Melissa's directions, but she doesn't have the chocolate, so I don't know how to do it."

"I'm reading my writing and Nicole is doing my directions but she's not *doing* them."

"I CAN'T! I don't have the chocolate!"

Name what the children have already done as writers.

"I can see you guys are frustrated, but you know what? You are trying to do something really smart—testing out the directions to see if they work. You are right, Nicole, the two of you have a tricky challenge because you can't really, truly, test out the directions unless you go over to each other's houses and do the cooking for real, with the chocolate and the stove and everything!"

It is interesting to notice that in this unit many of the conferences include a teacher coaching into the work of partners! This wasn't planned, and it is worth speculating whether this comes about because the unit is late in the year or whether there is something about nonfiction writing that supports peer collaboration.

Psychotherapists are taught that it can help to say back what a client says. "I hear you are really angry at your mother," the therapist says. Here, as the teacher, I use the same strategy of active listening. I say, "I hear that you are really frustrated. . . ."

Decide/Teach

Weigh whether you want to accept or alter the children's intentions. In this case, you decide to teach by demonstrating how writers and readers can generate a mental movie as they read to test a draft's clarity. Set the children up to learn from your demonstration by naming what you aim to do.

"Nicole, remember how in the minilesson I said that sometimes we are going to need to *pretend* that we are following the directions? Writers do this a lot. When I write about the ocean, I pretend that I am there so I can get the exact words down. I use my mind to imagine what it would be like. When any of us reads a story about an ocean, we need to create a picture in our minds, to see it stretching out before us. Today, let's both be readers and we'll listen to Melissa's directions and pretend we're making chocolate lollipops in our minds. Let's see if we can let the words help us create a picture (just like when we read about being at the ocean and create the picture). Let's try together, okay?"

Demonstrate to show the children what you hope they will soon do. In this case, show the children how to listen to the writer's directions while trying to envision each step. Think aloud so that when the directions are vague, your difficulties generating a "movie in your mind" are evident.

Speaking now to the writer, I said, "Melissa, would you read the directions step by step, and Nicole and I will follow your directions by making movies in our minds. Go slowly so we can imagine what your words are saying."

Melissa began. "Melt the chocolate." [*Fig. 10*]

I looked up into space as if trying to conjure up an image. "I'm having a hard time getting a picture in my mind. I can't make a picture of *how* to melt it. Do you put it in your hands like when you put snow in your hands and it melts?" Then I turned to her coreader and said, "How about you, Nicole? Do Melissa's words tell you enough to be able to imagine how to do this?"

Nicole said, "No. How does it melt? Do you light a fire?"

"You have to put the chocolate over hot water to melt it," Melissa clarified.

Notice that in this instance, as usual, I name what I will demonstrate before launching into the demonstration. I point out how I want Nicole and Melissa to listen.

Often, when the method we select is "explicitly tell," we rely on a metaphor to make our point.

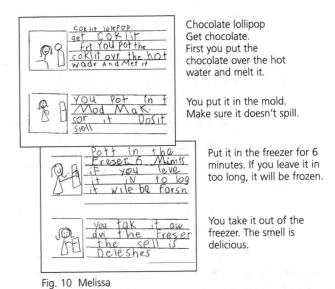

Chocolate lollipop
Get chocolate.
First you put the chocolate over the hot water and melt it.

You put it in the mold. Make sure it doesn't spill.

Put it in the freezer for 6 minutes. If you leave it in too long, it will be frozen.

You take it out of the freezer. The smell is delicious.

Fig. 10 Melissa

I don't simply summarize the fact that it was hard for me to envision what Melissa hopes her text suggests, I reenact my effort to visualize. I hope Melissa empathizes when I run into difficulty as I try to create a movie in my mind.

"OH! Now I can picture how you do it! First you put the chocolate over the hot water and that is how you melt it," I restated the first step in Melissa's directions, adding in the new information.

Help the children get started doing what you have demonstrated. In this case, help the writing partner listen to the writer's directions while trying to envision what those directions are suggesting a reader/listener do.

"Melissa, keep reading. Read the next step. As she reads it, I said, "Nicole, try to imagine what her words are saying in your mind. Then you can tell Melissa what you see and she can check whether her directions are doing the job." Then I nodded for Melissa to continue her blow-by-blow progress through the text. "What's next, Melissa?"

Melissa continued, "Put the melted chocolate in the mold."

"Okay, Nicole, do you have a picture in your mind? What are you seeing?"

"I'm pouring it in. It is spilling all over."

"Good job, Nicole. You are envisioning the words that Melissa is saying to you."

"Wait," Melissa added, "You have to get a spoon and put the chocolate in the mold slowly with a spoon."

"What a smart revision you just thought of! Later, you better put that down!"

Take the writer back to the beginning of the process you have demonstrated and help her get started putting her revisions on the page.

"So, Melissa. Now you need to go back and reread your first page, trying to make a movie in your mind of it—'Melt the chocolate'—and see if you can remember what you need to do differently on that first page so that readers will be able to make a movie in their minds of the whole thing. Then reread the next page, and so on."

Link

Ask the children to name what they have done as writers, and then remind them to do this often in future writing.

"So, Nicole and Melissa, any time you want to see if the words you or someone else has written really work, read them and see if you can get a picture in your mind."

Actually, of course, Melissa hasn't yet really clarified how this happens. Does one hold a candy bar in the air over the hot water faucet? But my point isn't to use this conference to make Melissa's writing perfect. These are young children. I mostly want Melissa to try to be more specific so her audience can follow what she says. I know from the start that children of this age will make only a certain amount of progress towards writing explicit, clear directions.

It is always the case that if demonstration is oral, once this work is over the writer will have to go back to the beginning of her text to make any suggested improvements. This can pose organizational challenges for writers, so help them out. Take the child or the children back to the start of the sequence of work you are trying to set them up to do.

"What Will You Write in Your Table of Contents?"

PROCESS AND GOALS CONFERENCE
METHOD: Demonstrate

Teach a child to anticipate subtopics and write them as chapter headings in a table of contents.

Research

Observe and interview to understand what the child is trying to do as a writer and as a student of nonfiction writing. In this case, the child chose table of contents paper quickly but has not yet written anything on it.

Amanda noticed that Christine was one of the first children to pick up table of contents paper. She was surprised, however, five minutes later, to see that Christine's paper was still blank. [*Fig. 11*] Amanda decided to see what was preventing her from progressing.

"What work are you doing as a writer today?" Amanda asked as she drew her chair alongside Christine's desk.

"I'm trying to write my table of contents," Christine answered, gesturing towards her paper.

Name what the child has done as a writer, and remind her to do this often in future writing.

"Christine, I love the way that you got started today. You got your paper and tools so quickly. And you chose to work on your table of contents. You must already have some ideas about what you are going to write! What are you thinking about putting into your table of contents?"

Christine shook her head to suggest that no, she *didn't* actually have ideas for what to write on this page. "I'm thinking still," she explained.

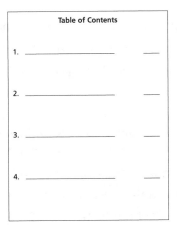

Fig. 11   Table of Contents paper

It is much easier to confer well with a child if that child has told us her intention. Our job, then, becomes providing requested help.

This is a very typical response for young children when they don't understand what to do. If a child is truly weighing one option and then another, that child is apt to say his or her thoughts. When a child says, "I'm thinking," that "thinking" often amounts to mental paralysis.

Decide/Teach

Weigh whether you want to accept or alter the child's intentions. In this case, you decide to teach by demonstrating how a table of contents page helps writers organize information. Set the child up to learn from your demonstration by naming what you aim to do.

"Let me show you how you might decide on some chapters you could include in your table of contents," Amanda said. Christine's answer was in her eyes. She nodded with great enthusiasm, as if she'd had a sudden burst of sugar energy.

Demonstrate to the child what you hope she will soon do. In this case, show the child how to list different chapters of a nonfiction piece across her fingers.

"First I try and remember different parts of my topic. I list the different parts, the different chapters, across my fingers. Let me think . . ." Amanda made her hand into a fist. "Let me think what is my topic about. Oh yeah, frogs! Now let me use my fingers to think of the chapters," Amanda raised one finger slowly, "Let's see, Chapter 1, Different kinds of frogs." Then she raised a second finger, "Chapter 2, Where they live." Then she raised finger number three, and said, "Chapter 3, How to take care of a pet frog." Then she stopped and looked at her three fingers. "Did you see how each finger is a different chapter? Those would be the titles that I write in my table of contents."

Amanda has made her case and doesn't need to continue with a longer and longer list. Notice that Amanda reenacts this in a blow-by-blow fashion, as is required for a demonstration, rather than simply summarizing the chain of events.

Help the child get started doing what you have just demonstrated

"I know your topic is horses, not frogs, so try it with horses," Amanda said.

Christine looked ready for the challenge. Before Christine began, Amanda prompted her, saying, "Get your fingers ready and think about your topic." Amanda put her hand out so that she would be ready to join Christine as she tried to use this strategy.

Christine started talking. "I know a lot about horses 'cause I ride horses, so I can tell kids how."

Notice that again, we take time to set a child up for success with whatever we ask the child to do.

As Christine said this, Amanda held up the corresponding finger. "So that's a chapter, Christine! 'How to ride a horse.' What else have you and Rebecca talked about as possible chapters for your book?"

"Special clothes to wear," Christine said. Amanda looked at Christine's fingers as if waiting expectantly for her to register that this the suggested title for Chapter 2. Christine followed Amanda's gaze and moved her second finger up.

"Different colors of horses," Christine continued and lifted her third finger.

"Did you hear what you just said? Each of the things you are listing could be the chapters that you put into your table of contents page."

Link

Name what the child has done as a writer, and remind her to do this often in future writing. Set her up to continue working.

"Christine, whenever you are stuck on what sections you might include in an All-About book, tell your friend what you plan to write and then stop and say, 'Wait, the things I'm saying— they can each be chapters!' Our fingers can help us plan how the chapters in our nonfiction books will go, so that we can write those chapters' names in our table of contents. Okay, let me watch you get started." Christine looked at her paper and then up at Amanda again.

Giving her another nudge, Amanda said, "So now, Christine, take your table of contents paper, say the things you mentioned when you were trying on your topic, and then decide if each of those things could be a chapter in your book." Amanda then asked, "What was the first thing? Was it 'How to ride a horse'?"

Christine nodded and started writing.

The fingers act as very effective graphic organizers. They help children get into the habit of listing separate but parallel items. Notice that Amanda restates Christine's point so that it is clearly a How-To subtopic.

It is wise of Amanda to say nothing, but to stick up a second finger. Amanda is right there with Christine but she lets Christine rework with as little support (and interference) as necessary.

Watch the way Amanda takes Christine back to the start and gets her up and going.

PROCESS AND GOALS CONFERENCE
METHOD: Demonstrate

Teach a child to punctuate to make the meaning clear.

Research

Observe, interview, and read the child's writing to understand what the child is trying to do as a writer and as a student of nonfiction writing. In this case, the child is engaged in working on an All-About book.

Amanda watched Mohammed as he finished page two of his book about basketball. She pulled her chair up next to him and watched as he worked his way down his page. After he completed each sentence, Mohammed lifted his pencil from the page, and looked as if he was thinking of the next thing. Once he got an idea, he'd bring his pencil back to the page, write *and,* and be off and running with his next sentence.

"How's it going, Mohammed?"

"Good," he said as he continued writing.

"Yeah?" Amanda said, and then paused, waiting for Mohammed's attention.

"Yep. It's good." Mohammed said. "I'm on my third page. I'm writing about basketball. Now I am writing about the positions on a basketball team."

"That seems important."

"It is. I like to play guard. But you need five people for your team."

"Mohammed, you have a ton to say about basketball, don't you?"

This moment of observation goes a long way toward informing Amanda about Mohammed's progress as a writer. It wasn't long ago that Mohammed only wrote one sentence on a page, and it is clear to Amanda that he's developed a lot more stamina as a writer. She also knows that although he has a felt sense for when a sentence ends, he prefers to use conjunctions rather than end punctuation. It is almost as if Mohammed wants to convey to his readers, "Wait! Wait! Don't stop. My writing keeps going."

Don't continue talking if the child doesn't pause and look up at you. You want to signal to children that these conversations are of the utmost importance—the message is altogether wrong if a child doesn't even need to attend to you.

"Well, next I am going to write about the NBA, but that's gonna go on the other paper. 'Cause this paper is named [and he pointed to the heading at the top of his page] *Posishuns on a Team*. And after that, I'm gonna tell about the shoes they wear."

Name what the child has already done as a writer, and remind him to do this often in future writing.

"It is really smart that you have plans for your writing. I love the way that you know exactly what your work will be for the next couple of days, and you even know what paper will hold which chapter. To me, it feels like you have really made this into your own project—you have so many ideas for how it will go! That's great."

Study the draft to glean more about the child's intentions.

"May I just look quickly at your writing?" Amanda took a quick tour over his first two pages to see if there was a pattern in his writing. She saw, as she'd suspected from the start of the conference, that Mohammed rarely used end punctuation except at the very end of a page. Earlier in the year, run-on sentences had not been an issue for Mohammed.

Decide/Teach

Weigh whether you want to accept or alter the child's intentions. In this case, the child has direction and energy for the next steps in his writing and so you decide to demonstrate how much easier his writing would be to read if it included end punctuation. Set the child up to learn from your demonstration by naming what you aim to do.

"Mohammed, I think you're doing a great job writing all about basketball—you don't need my help with that. But especially because you are writing this important, long book, you want to make sure people can read it. I want to give you one tip as a writer before you get back to work: Writers use a period at the end of each sentence to show when the reader needs to pause. I want to you to watch me now, because I'm going to show you how writers do this."

You might be tempted to teach a child to focus, narrowing down his topic, and you could do that with very advanced writers if you get to them early enough that they don't have to discard much of their hard work. But with most of your students, you will probably need to let go of the urge to have them write lovely, focused prose and be satisfied if their writing is categorized and clear and informative. Expect a lot of lists and a lot of underdeveloped writing.

Don't be surprised to see that children go two steps forward and one step back. It makes sense that Mohammed, who had previously been writing very brief pieces involving a single sentence on each page of a book and who now was writing many sentences across each of his pages, would become temporarily mired in run-on sentences. The fact that run-on sentences are prevalent now in his writing is a reflection of Mohammed's growing stamina and his commitment to his topic. They are growing pains.

In this conference, Amanda takes control of the conference agenda to bring Mohammed's attention to a point she decides is important. The nice thing about this is that Amanda owns up to this and lets Mohammed know it isn't "business as usual."

Demonstrate to the child what he tends to do in writing. In this case, the child tends to omit end punctuation.

"What you do now, Mohammed, is you write like this," Amanda took a white board and a marker and began to write:

Every basketball team needs five players

Amanda looked up, showing Mohammed she was deep in thought, and then said, "Oh, yeah!" She tucked her head back towards the board and added on another idea. She did this again and at the end of the new sentence, so that soon her writing looked like this:

Every basketball team needs five players and three players on the basketball team are the forwards and one player on the team is the center forward. . . .

Mohammed smiled at Amanda as she worked, as if beginning to catch on to what she was showing him. When she read her piece out loud without any pauses between sentences, he giggled with delight and said, "That's no good! There's no breaths!"

Demonstrate what you hope the writer will soon do. In this case, show the child how writers add a period at the end of a sentence.

"Smart observation, Mohammed. Now let me show you what I mean by writing with periods. Watch how I do it. Okay, I'm going to write about basketball." Amanda took up the marker and this is what she wrote:

Every basketball team needs five players

Amanda paused and looked up, as before, but this time she said, "period" out loud before adding the period to her sentence.

Then Amanda questioned herself, "What should I say next?"

Soon she was writing again, but before she started, she reminded herself under her breath, for Mohammed's benefit, "I just wrote a period so I now I need to start with a capital letter."

Notice that Amanda doesn't just talk about punctuation. She shows Mohammed the process of writing without periods and with periods. Almost always, it works to act out what we're trying to teach.

In life, it is a great gift if someone helps us realize what we tend to do, and even better if the person shows us how we could be more effective by altering our way of doing things. Amanda is helpful when she says to Mohammed, "This is what you tend to do." Meanwhile she is doing more than merely assigning Mohammed to write with periods. She is trying to teach him a strategy for doing so.

Soon the text looked like this:

Every basketball team needs five players. Three players on the team are the forwards. One player on the team is the center forward.

When Amanda read the piece to Mohammed this time, there was plenty of time to breathe between sentences. "Did you see what I did?" she asked him. "I wrote my sentence, I paused, I reminded myself about the period, and I kept going."

"Yep, I saw," said Mohammed.

Help the child get started doing what you have just demonstrated.

"When you write, Mohammed, what I notice is that you usually pause and look up. When you pause and look up, use that time to remind yourself about the periods. Read back what you wrote to see if it makes sense and then figure out what comes next. Let's try."

Mohammed had already written, "Every team needs five people." Then he paused and looked at Amanda, as if asking, "Is now the time?"

Amanda nodded, and Mohammed wrote a period. "Now read it back." Mohammed read it back. "Keep going."

Mohammed wrote, "You need one guard." When he said the last word, he paused and was about to write something else but then stopped. He yelled out, "Period!"

Link

Name what the child has done as a writer, and remind him to do this often in future writing. Set him up to continue working.

"I like the way you are thinking about periods! Saying 'period' out loud isn't a bad idea—for now, this might help you as you write. You definitely need to keep adding periods to this piece. When you get to the end of the page, reread the entire piece and check for your periods."

The rhythm in conferences is very much the same whether we are teaching a child to notice and emulate an author's craft techniques or to use end punctuation.

Amanda wants to see how he will handle it without scaffolding or prompting.

PART SEVEN

POETRY: POWERFUL THOUGHTS IN TINY PACKAGES

In this unit, as in the nonfiction unit, you'll draw on your entire repertoire of conferences. One difference is that your children will not move in sync during this unit, meaning that as you move among children, you'll help one to plan and envision a poem, the next to edit the poem to make it readable, the next to emulate techniques a writer has used. This unit of study, then, will put high demands on you as a teacher of writing. It's perfect that this comes after the other units!

The other challenge you'll face is that you will want to invest a lot of time and attention into teaching children qualities of good writing. It won't be enough to show children that they can rework their ending . . . what makes for effective endings in a poem? It won't be enough for children to add details—how can they select details that will be powerful ones?

Your conferences will be vastly more powerful if your pockets are full of information and insights about effective poetry. Try reading Georgia Heard's For the Good of The Earth and the Sun, and carrying some of that information—plus your knowledge of conferences—with you as you confer. Be outspoken that you, too, are learning about poetry. "I've been reading a book about poetry, and one thing I've learned that you might try is. . . ."

Remember, too, that what all of us need most as writers are readers who listen deeply, and who let our words affect them. Reread the child's draft. Read it aloud like it is precious. Take it in. Let it matter. Gasp. Envision. Cherish a line, an image. Your human response will matter more than anything.

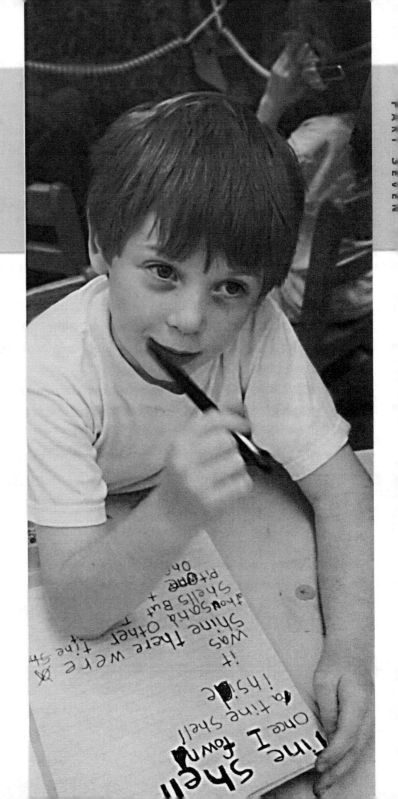

PROCESS AND GOALS CONFERENCE
METHODS: Explicitly Tell, Guided Practice

Teach a child to focus her big feeling around a specific moment.

Research

Observe and interview to understand what the child is trying to do as a poet. In this case, Khalea is planning her poem.

Before Stephanie approached, Khalea was staring dreamily towards the ceiling. She had not yet started writing, although writing workshop had been in full force for at least ten minutes. Stephanie watched for a moment, then knelt down beside her.

"Khalea?" Khalea hardly looked at Stephanie, choosing instead to continue tapping her pencil, looking as if she was lost in thought.

Name what the child has already done, and remind her to do the same in the future.

"Khalea, I can tell you are really thinking! You are looking just like a poet—thinking, thinking, getting ready to put the poem on the paper!" Khalea smiled but didn't respond.

Probe to glean more about the child's intentions.

"Have you found the start to a poem?"

"I don't know 'cause I have a feeling of 'I like the ocean' but I don't know how to get a poem."

Stephanie is giving Khalea the benefit of the doubt. "I can tell you are really thinking, thinking," she says. "You are looking like a poet. . . ." Early on in a unit we do all we can to recruit children's enthusiasm for the work that lies ahead. This often includes finding ways for them to role-play their way into being the writers we want them to be.

Decide/Teach

Weigh whether you want to accept or alter the child's intentions. In this case, decide to help Khalea focus her big feeling about the ocean on one particular moment. Teach by explicitly telling this to the writer, and then by giving her guided practice in locating her big feeling in a specific moment.

"Ah ha," said Stephanie. "You know, grownup poets have that same trouble. Sometimes the feeling is so big, and there are so many different ways you could write it—it can be overwhelming, huh?"

"Yup," she nodded. "I get so frustrated because I know I have a big topic."

"Well, Khalea, one thing that poets do when we have a big feeling but aren't sure where the poem starts, or how it starts, is that we fill ourselves full of that big feeling—like you with the ocean—and then think of a particular moment when we had that very same feeling. It's easier sometimes to start the poem if you focus on one little moment—the little moment is like a handle for the big feeling." Khalea stared at Stephanie thoughtfully.

When teaching poetry, sometimes our teaching language becomes more poetic. It is as if no ordinary words will do the trick. We need to think, perceive, and explain things with the same sense of poetry that writers are now thinking and perceiving with. In short, we need to speak the poet's language to effectively convey what we mean.

Help the writer get started doing what you hope she will do.

"Khalea, do you think you could get that feeling of loving the ocean in you right now? Can you feel how much you love the ocean? How it feels when you see it, smell it, feel the waves moving your body around? Can you remember being at the ocean, and can you get that 'I'm at the ocean' feeling in your chest, right this minute?"

Khalea scrunched up her face and puffed up her chest as if the feeling she wanted to contain was making her very full indeed.

Trust in details. Use them in your teaching. Instead of talking in generalizations about sensory details, get down to the level of detail, even if this means you sort of take-over-a-bit-of-the-child's-topic for a minute. Stephanie is doing a tiny bit of demonstration here, showing Khalea what it is like to fill oneself with that "I'm at the ocean" feeling.

Interject lean prompts that scaffold the child in a step-by-step fashion.

"Now you need to go to one small, particular time when you were at the ocean. Remember one? Remember where you stood, or swam, or ran? See the ocean, and hear it, and smell it—all with that big feeling in your heart that you started out with. Tell me exactly what you see."

"It's quiet. The quiet ocean." She paused and continued, "Fish are swimming. And they are quiet. . . ."

Pause to give her time to generate the memory of a particular moment.

"Is the water quiet, too?" Stephanie prompted, as Khalea paused, uncertain.

"No," said Khalea, eyes squinched tight. "The waves are swishing and the water makes splash noises."

Take the child back to the beginning of what she has said, and help her get started recording that. Tell the writer that she must record what she has said onto the page.

"Khalea, that is beautiful. I hope you write that down, what you just said about the quiet fish and the swishing waves! And when you've finished, I hope you keep going—keep thinking about this specific time at the ocean. I'll come back to check on you in a few minutes, okay?" Khalea nodded and began writing.

After a conference with another child, Stephanie returned to check on Khalea. Figure 12 shows Khalea's writing.

Link

Name what the child has done, and remind her to do this often in the future.

"Khalea, I am in awe of this poem. You did something amazing here—you took that strong feeling you had about the ocean and filled yourself up with it—then you thought about one specific time when you were there, and you started writing exactly what you saw and heard. From now on, remember to do what you did today when you aren't sure how to get started on your poem."

Be conscious of your voice. Let it convey majesty and awe. Speak more quietly than the child.

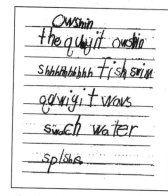

Ocean
The quiet ocean
Shhh fish swim
Quiet waves
Swash water
Splashes

Fig. 12   Khalea

"ARE THOSE THE SOUNDS YOU HEAR?"

PROCESS AND GOALS CONFERENCE
METHOD: Guided Practice

Teach a child to say the words and then write down only the sounds she actually hears.

Research

Observe and interview to understand what the child is trying to do as a poet. In this case, the child is engaged in writing her poem about eating ice cream in the summertime.

Though Stephanie decided to confer with Anna about her spelling, she still need to research Anna's specific needs as a speller, decide what to teach her, and then teach it.

Stephanie pulled up a chair and read Anna's poem over her shoulder. [*Fig. 13*]

Stephanie has plenty of possible teaching points she could make to support Anna's spelling. Before considering them, she notices what Anna is doing well as a speller: spelling several sight words correctly, spelling -ing correctly, and using some initial blends (cr- in cream and dr- in dribbles).

Based on this, Stephanie thinks about some of the things Anna is ready to work on the -er ending (as in summer), choosing the right short vowel (as in melting, dribbles, and lick), more initial blends (as in still), more known spelling patterns (as in hand, eat, ice, or lick), or that troublesome a that appears at the end of some words when a child sounds out words with a big old schwa at the end, even though there's none there. Can you practically hear it? "Summ-er-ah."

It is summer!
I am eating
ice cream
I take big
bites!
But it still
is melting
it dribbles
on my
hand
and
I lick
it

Fig. 13   Anna

Name what the child has done as a writer, and remind her to do this often in future writing.

"Anna, it's great to see you over here so busy with your poem. It looks like the world of your poem is really in your head right now—I don't even think you noticed me sitting here!" She smiled.

With the exception of that a, all the issues above are pretty widespread in the classroom and can be addressed in minilessons, strategy lessons, or word study. Anna will get more out of a conference that deals with an issue particular to her.

Decide/Teach

Weigh whether you want to accept or alter the child's intentions. In this case, decide to help the child write down only the sounds she hears in words she is stretching out. Teach by providing her with guided practice in saying a word, writing the sounds she hears, and rereading often.

Notice that Stephanie doesn't really do her usual research. She cuts short that phase.

"You know, Anna, I've noticed something that you do in your spelling that's not helping you or your readers—and I think you're ready to tackle it! You are so careful when you sound out words, which is good. But sometimes maybe you are a little *too* careful, and you put in some extra sounds that aren't really there." Anna looked up at Stephanie quizzically.

"Listen to this word: *summer*. What do you hear at the very end?"

"*Ssss-uuuuuuh-mmmmm-errrrrrrruh*," said Anna.

It's helpful to be as direct and clear as possible. Stephanie wastes no time getting to her point.

Help the writer get started doing what you hope she will do. In this case, help the child say the word normally to help her write down the sounds in that word.

"Okay, now just say *summer* instead of sounding it out—writers do that when they want to hear and write down only the sounds that are really there in the word."

"*Summer.*"

"Good. What did you hear?"

"/Mer/."

It's hard for kids to isolate the ending sound from the rest of the word. Anna had to hear the end by getting through the sounds at the beginning of the word first. "Sssss-uuuuh-mmmm-errrrruh."

Interject lean, efficient prompts to scaffold the child's work in a step-by-step fashion.

"Excellent! Me too! So what's at the end of /mer/?"

"/Er/. Oh, it's an *r*, not an *a*!"

"Anna, it totally and completely *is* an *r*. Good listening. Sometimes it's easier to hear a sound when you just say the word normally than it is when you stretch it way out. So what do you think is at the end of, say, *teacher*?"

"An *r*?"

"Yes! What about *weather*?"

"*R*." Anna made the correction on her paper.

Let the intervals between your prompts become longer as the child becomes accustomed to the process and is able to continue with less support.

"Yes, yes, yes. So listen. When you are trying to spell a word that ends that way, with an /er/ sound, instead of stretching out the whole word, you can just know that it ends in *r*. Okay?"

"Okay."

Link

Name what the child has done, and remind her to do this often in the future. Set her up to continue working.

"Good. Now down here, the word *bites* has the same problem. I'm going to leave you alone to try this whole thing again with this word, and I'm going to come back in a few minutes and see how it's going. Remember to say the word normally and see if that helps you hear the ending better."

Stephanie doesn't progress to new spelling pointers but instead gives Anna ample chances to practice the one thing she's just learned.

It's helpful to set the child up to continue doing what you've just taught her to do.

PROCESS AND GOALS CONFERENCE
METHOD: Guided Practice

Teach a child to develop a poem by showing, not telling.

Research

Observe, interview, and read the child's writing to understand what the child is trying to do as a poet. In this case, the child is rereading a poem he started yesterday.

I watched Ramon as he got out his poetry folder, looked through it, and selected the piece he had started yesterday. Ramon is full of ideas, and his folder is stuffed with the beginnings of poems. I was pleased to see that he was returning to yesterday's draft to do more work on it. I approached and watched him rereading the poem to himself.

Name what the child has already done as a writer, and remind him to do this often in the future.

After a moment, I said, "Ramon, that is so cool how you chose a poem to work on today and started rereading it right away. You sure know how to get yourself ready to work!"

Probe to learn more about the child's intentions.

"What do you think your writing work for today will be?"

"Oh, I just like this poem I did yesterday. It's all done. I like it! I'm gonna do another poem today, about. . . ."

"Ramon, I'm going to stop you for a second—keep that new thought for later, I bet it's a great one—but right now I want to look some more with you at the poem you started yesterday."

Matter-of-factly, I said, "You know, poets stay with their poems for a long time, to make sure they are exactly how they want them to be. Especially if the poems grow out of ideas that you really, really care about. I know you care about this one!" Ramon looked at me with obvious annoyance, like a little

Remember that research begins when we sit alongside a child and watch what he or she does. It's helpful to train yourself to notice what a child does that merits celebration because our human instinct is often to search for flaws.

While I was listening to Ramon's explanation I knew I wanted to help him stay with the draft he was working on. I didn't want him to launch into one of his wildly imaginative descriptions of what he could do next. Instead, I wanted him to return to the draft he'd selected and to make it better.

racehorse bursting to get out of the stall. I wanted to get him into this work as quickly as possible. "Ramon, can you read me your poem from yesterday?"

He tucked his head and read aloud. [*Fig. 14*]

Name what the child has done as a writer, and remind him to do this often in future writing.

"Ramon, wow! I love this tiny little moment you have captured in your poem! You are thinking like a poet! I can really see the boy sprinkling bits of bread to the birds—you did a great job right there showing, not telling, like poets do."

"Yep," said Ramon, sure of his poetry prowess.

Decide/Teach

Weigh whether you want to accept or alter the child's current process. In this case, decide to teach the child to make this poem even better by using "show, not tell" in more parts of the poem. Teach by showing the child an example of his own work, and then by providing him with guided practice in "showing, not telling."

"One thing I'm thinking, though, is that you could do even more of the great work you've already done on this poem, so that we readers can see even more of what you saw out the window at Daniel's house. Because you were thinking about showing and not telling right here," I pointed to the bread-sprinkling line, "I can imagine the boy sprinkling the bread, but not much else. You know, poets often go back to poems they have already started to make sure that they are doing their best to show, not tell *all* about their idea."

Help the writer get started doing what you hope he will soon do. In this case, help the child imagine himself into the context of his poem to recall details that show, instead of tell.

"I want you to try that right now—imagine that moment again—what exactly did you see out the window? What did the birds do when they got the bread? How many birds were there? See *everything* that you saw out the window!" Ramon willingly closed his eyes. I could see them moving around under the lids, as if he was really looking.

So often, children think poetry must be about rainbows and love. It is refreshing to see this child try to capture a glimpse of a boy feeding birds in his poem.

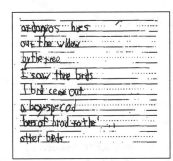

At Daniel's house out the window by the tree I saw three birds. A boy sprinkled bits of bread to the other birds.

Fig. 14 Ramon

Sometimes, our instinct is to notice what a child has done well and then teach something different. Another option is to extend what the child has done well, encouraging the child to do that often.

Instead of just telling Ramon to show, not tell, I try to give him the strategies he needs to pull this off. I don't, of course, know how others go about showing rather than telling, so what I do is to name the strategies I use, and help Ramon try them.

Interject lean, efficient prompts to scaffold the child's work in a step-by-step fashion.

He smiled suddenly, and I said, "Okay, Ramon, what did you see? What else can you put into your poem so that you are showing, not telling what happened out the window?"

"Well, it was so funny, when the boy sprinkled the bread, the birds were sort of like they were laughing!"

"What do you mean they were laughing? Say more. . . ."

"Well it was like their heads were just jumping up and down, and then one guy put his head down on his chest, like this. . . . "

Ramon demonstrated, tucking his small chin down onto his chest, keeping his brown eyes focused on me.

Let the intervals between your prompts become longer as the child becomes accustomed to the process and is able to continue with less support.

"Wow, Ramon, that is amazing. I can see so much more of what you saw out the window. You have *got* to put that into your poem! How will you add your new thinking?"

"I think I can just put it down at the bottom of here," he points to some empty space at the bottom of his first draft, "about how the birds were laughing."

Link

Name what the child has done as a writer, and remind him to do this often in future writing. Set him up to continue working.

"Great Ramon, get started. Remember that you can do this always, you can go back to a poem that you already started to make sure you did everything you could do to show, not tell about your idea. I'm going to come check on you in a few minutes, okay?"

When I returned close to the end of the workshop, Ramon had added to his writing. [*Fig. 15*]

Again, I need to take Ramon back to the beginning and help him get started.

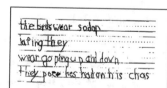

the birds were sort of
laughing they
were jumping up and down
they put his head on his chest

Fig. 15   Ramon